DISCO
DRINKS

60 Decadent and Delicious Cocktails, Pitcher Drinks, and No/Lo Sippers

JASSY DAVIS

ROCK
POINT

This book is for Nicola Swift, the originator of Nana Disco

© 2023 by Quarto Publishing Group USA Inc.

Jassy Davis asserts the moral right to be identified as the author of this work.

This edition published in 2023 by Rock Point, an imprint of The Quarto Group,
142 West 36th Street, 4th Floor, New York, NY 10018, USA
T (212) 779-4972 F (212) 779-6058
www.Quarto.com

First published in Great Britain by HarperCollinsPublishers Ltd 2023
1 London Bridge Street
London SE1 9GF
www.harpercollins.co.uk

Rock Point titles are also available at discount for retail, wholesale, promotional, and bulk purchase. For details, contact the Special Sales Manager by email at specialsales@quarto.com or by mail at The Quarto Group, Attn: Special Sales Manager, 100 Cummings Center Suite 265D, Beverly, MA 01915 USA.

10 9 8 7 6 5 4 3 2 1

ISBN: 978-1-63106-982-6

Library of Congress Control Number: 2023935954

Group Publisher: Rage Kindelsperger
Creative Director: Laura Drew
Managing Editor: Cara Donaldson
HarperCollins Editor: Caitlin Doyle
Cover and Interior Design: Jacqui Caulton
Text: Jassy Davis

Printed in Latvia

DISCO DRINKS is intended only for responsible adults of legal drinking age in the United States of America (21 years old or older). Please do NOT drink and drive. If you need transportation, use a designated driver or a taxi service. And please be careful when crossing the street after drinking.

DISCO DRINKS does not advocate or encourage the abuse of alcoholic beverages. Please drink responsibly and in moderation. We do not, under any circumstances, accept responsibility for any damages that result to yourself or anyone else due to the consumption of alcoholic beverages or the use of this book and any materials located in it. We cannot take any responsibility for the effect these drinks may have on people. As such, we do not accept liability for any loss, damage, or inconvenience that occurs as a result of the use of this book or your reliance upon its content.

This book features recipes that include the optional use of raw eggs. Consuming raw eggs may increase the risk of food-borne illness. Individuals who are immunocompromised, pregnant, or elderly should use caution.
Ensure eggs are fresh and meet local food-standard requirements.

CONTENTS

WELCOME

Everybody needs a little more disco in their life—more fun, more strut, more swagger, more glamour, and lots more joy. The spirit of disco is vibrant and carefree, while the drinks that defined that era are full of bright colors and bold flavors. They're the cocktails that aren't afraid to be fun.

Whether they're long and fruity or short and creamy, a disco drink is always beautifully made and garnished. You'll find guides to buying the best glassware and making gorgeous garnishes in this book, along with a chapter on the key techniques you'll need to stir up cocktails that will always impress.

There are recipes for disco classics, like neon-bright Blue Hawaiis, blushing Pink Squirrels, and Japanese Slippers—audacious drinks that demand to be admired. Decadent and indulgent Brandy Alexanders, Grasshoppers, and White Russians make no apologies for their richness, while Piña Coladas, Tequila Sunrises, and Sloe Comfortable Screws are happiness in a glass.

But disco drinks aren't only about the 1970s and '80s. Camp classics like the Espresso Martini, Pornstar Martini, Cosmopolitan, and the Shark Bite are all infused with disco's playfulness, which has continued long after the original disco age ended. They're drinks that don't take themselves too seriously, love a bit of drama, and are here to have fun. This book brings them all together, along with original drinks inspired by the look, feel, and flavor of the disco age.

You'll find a mix of single serves and plenty of pitcher drinks in this book, as well as nonalcoholic options. While you can of course throw a bedroom disco for one, a party vibe is always best when it's shared. So, grab your friends and your cocktail shaker—it's time to celebrate!

Each recipe features a color key (examples below) to indicate whether the flavor profile is tropical, smoky, sweet, fizzy, etc.

 Tropical   Smoky   Sweet   Fizzy

TOOLS AND EQUIPMENT

Getting Started

Disco is for everybody, whether you've got a range of vintage shaking tins and etched mixing glasses or you're making do with a pitcher, a wooden spoon, and a lidded glass jar. This guide to setting up your own home bar will help you work out what you need, what you want, and what you already have.

COCKTAIL SHAKER

A cocktail shaker quickly chills your drink while diluting it. This is a crucial step when mixing drinks, as it mellows the alcohol and makes the finished drink smoother. Shakers also give cocktails life. The first sip of a shaken drink should fill your mouth with texture and sparkle. Plus, shaking cocktails looks cool, so a cocktail shaker is a fun thing to own.

There are three basic cocktail shakers to choose from: the Boston shaker, the cobbler shaker, and the French shaker.

- **Boston shaker:** This is the classic two-piece shaker that you'll typically see in bars. It consists of a large shaking tin and a smaller

tin, also known as a pint glass. The upside to the Boston shaker is that it's big, giving the ice and drink plenty of room to move and aerate. The downside is that it can be tricky to seal and open; expect spills when you start learning how to use it. You'll also need to buy a separate strainer.

- **Cobbler shaker:** A three-piece shaker with everything you need included. There's a tin, a lid with a built-in strainer, and a cap to cover it. This is perfect for beginners and you can normally use it to shake one- to two-person cocktails, or up to four shooters.

- **French shaker:** This is a halfway house between the Boston and the cobbler shakers. It has a tin and a lid but no built-in strainer, so you'll need to get a separate strainer to pour a smooth drink. It looks very sleek. If you want something that looks a little cooler than a cobbler but haven't worked up the courage to tackle a Boston shaker, this is a good option.

Not keen to shell out money for a shaker just yet? Then what you need is a jar. A mason jar, a Kilner jar, or even a well-scrubbed lidded glass jar or spaghetti sauce jar will make a decent stand-in for a cocktail shaker.

MIXING GLASSES

When you want to stir rather than shake a cocktail, you need a mixing glass. Typically, you'll use it to mix cocktails that are all liquor, although there are exceptions to this rule.

An all-booze mixed drink should have a silky texture and a spirit-forward flavor. So when you're picking your mixing glass, go for one that's wide enough to let you keep the bar spoon moving, and deep enough to contain the cocktail without it spilling over the top. A heavy base is more stable. You don't want it to topple over if you get a bit carried away. Etched mixing glasses can provide extra grip, and glasses with thick sides will insulate the drink from your hands. A mixing glass with a spout is significantly easier to pour from than one without—don't underestimate that fact.

An alternative you probably already have in your kitchen is an old-fashioned ovenproof glass pitcher. Thick, sturdy, and with that all-important spout, you can mix a solid Martini or Manhattan in one. You can also use the tin from your cocktail shaker, but be ready to deal with the consequences of the smooth, slippy sides and the lack of spout.

BAR SPOON

To go with your mixing glass, you'll need a bar spoon. These are long-stemmed spoons that typically have a ½ to 1 teaspoon bowl. There are three types of bar spoons: American, European, and Japanese.

- **American bar spoon:** The most simple, with a rubber cap on the end of the spoon and a twisted section in the middle. Great when you're starting out and just want something to stir drinks with.
- **European bar spoon:** This often has a round, flat disk at the end, which can be used to muddle soft fruits. The stem is twisted all the way down, and you can use it to layer drinks by trickling the liquor down the stem.
- **Japanese bar spoon:** This spoon tends to have teardrop- or pearl-shaped tip and is much longer than its American or European counterpart, making it a lot more theatrical and elegant to use.

No bar spoon at home? A dessert spoon is a bit clunky but you can get a swirl going with one. An ice cream sundae spoon would be better, but if you're buying sundae spoons then you may as well buy a bar spoon.

The handles of serving spoons can also work, and I have been known to use the handle of a wooden spoon when mixing drinks at parties (don't tell anyone I've done that).

JIGGER

A jigger is an hourglass-shaped measurer that has two measuring bowls—the standard jigger (1½ ounces) and the pony (1 ounce). These are the basic measurements for cocktail making.

You can also buy small measuring glasses that are marked up with ounces, tablespoons, and teaspoons, which I find helps with precision measuring.

If you don't mind getting a little Walter White, then a digital scale can save you some clean up time. Place your mixing glass or shaker tin on the scale, set the scale to zero, then slowly pour in your liquor. You do need a really steady hand for this, or the willingness to tolerate some generous overserves.

STRAINERS

A strainer is often useful, even if you're using a cobbler shaker, and it's non-negotiable for Boston shakers, French shakers, and mixing glasses. This is a bit of equipment you will have to invest in, so put it at the top of your shopping list.

A Hawthorne strainer is a metal disk with a coiled spring attached to it. It catches large chunks of fruit or ice when the cocktail is poured out. The Hawthorne strainer is perfect for straining cocktails from a shaking tin, and you can use it with your mixing glass too.

The traditional strainer for a mixing glass is a Julep strainer. It has a handle and is shaped like a bowl or spoon, but with holes stamped in it. The bowl shape of the strainer cups the ice in the glass, holding it back more firmly than a Hawthorne strainer and making it easier to pour your drink.

Sometimes a cocktail needs to be fine-strained or double-strained. This means you'll need to pour your cocktail through a Hawthorne or Julep strainer and also through a fine-mesh sieve in order to catch small pieces of fruit pulp, herbs, or chips of ice. Small, hand-held sieves, similar to tea strainers, work brilliantly for this.

MUDDLERS

Muddlers are used to crush soft fruits and herbs, lightly mash citrus peel to bring out the juices, crack seeds and nuts, and even crush ice (if you're feeling strong). Muddlers are usually made out of wood, plastic, or steel. Wood is the best-looking option, and pretty tough. Plastic and steel have the benefit of being dishwasher-friendly.

If you have a European bar spoon with a flat disk on the end of it, you don't need to buy a muddler as well. You can also use a pestle from your pestle and mortar, or the end of a rolling pin, if it's flat.

GARNISHING TOOLS

The secret to getting a perfect long strip of zest you can twist and twirl is a canele cutter or channel knife. These are narrow peelers that smoothly pull long ribbons of peel off an orange or lemon, which you can then turn into the perfect twist. If you have a zester at home, it probably has a v-shaped hole in the middle—that's a channel knife. Drag it sideways over a citrus fruit and you will get a good-looking strip of zest ready to twist.

You can also use a regular vegetable peeler to peel strips off citrus fruits, then use a small, sharp knife to neaten them up. The knife will also come in handy for slicing lemons and limes, or any other fruit you're using in your drinks.

A microplane grater is useful for grating nutmeg, chocolate, and zest. Finally, for picking up and placing very fine garnishes, a pair of long plating tongs will ensure everything ends up in the drink and not stuck to your fingers. These are a niche purchase and will sit low on your list of must-haves until you're truly cocktail obsessed.

JUICER

A big part of cocktail making is squeezing citrus fruits, so a lemon juicer is a handy bit of equipment to have in your cocktail cabinet.

BLENDERS

For frozen cocktails, a blender is essential. Choose a blender that's big enough and packs enough power—at least 1,000 watts. Blenders that promise they can crush ice and make smoothies are the best choice for cocktail making, as they're normally powerful and quick; the faster the blade spins, the finer your ingredients will be processed.

When it comes to making crushed ice, food processors usually do a better job than blenders, although the best crushed ice comes from the store.

ICE CUBE TRAYS

You're going to need plenty of ice. Buying bags of ice and crushed ice is quick, easy, and gives a great result. I pick up bags of ice from my local store for shaking and standard serves, then I have fun making more interesting ice cubes if I want a particular look.

Oversized ice cubes are great for shorter, spirit-forward drinks, like Old Fashioneds, while long, spear-shaped ice cubes can work in tall cocktails served in collins glasses. Really tiny ice cubes can look gorgeous and create a cobbled, pearly effect in the glass. And, of course, there's always space for fun ice cubes shaped like fish, hearts, diamonds, or whatever your imagination runs to.

DRINK POURERS

The most optional of all the bar equipment (apart from the plating tongs), a drink or cocktail pourer is a spout you fit to the top of your most-used spirits to make them easier to pour. Pourers allow for smooth, fast pouring and they reduce spillage. They're useful in bars when accuracy has to be matched with speed, but at home you don't need them unless you're looking to add some flair to your pours or you regularly have a crowd six-people deep at your home bar.

TRICKS AND TECHNIQUES

Throwing Shapes

Knowing how to use your barware with confidence will make sure you look good when you make drinks, whatever it is you're shaking.

HOW TO SHAKE

The most extroverted way to make a cocktail, shaking can be as big or small as you like. Just ensure you seal that shaker before you let fly.

COBBLER/FRENCH SHAKER

Add your cocktail ingredients to the base tin, then add enough ice to half-fill it. You can go up to two-thirds ice, if you like. Place the lid and cap on top of the tin and make sure they are tightly sealed.

Grip the base with one hand and use the other to hold the lid and cap, resting your fingers over the top to make sure it stays on. Shake vigorously, making sure the top is pointing mostly upwards and not at any people or nice bits of furniture—around 15–30 seconds will do it. When the tin feels frosty, it's ready.

Remove the cap, then pour the drink through the strainer, holding the shaker so your fingers keep the lid securely in place. If you're using a French shaker, remove the lid and use a Hawthorne strainer (see the Boston shaker method).

BOSTON SHAKER

Pour the ingredients into the smaller tin or glass and fill the larger tin with ice. Pick up the smaller tin and hold it over the larger tin at a slight angle so the liquids pour into the big tin, then invert the smaller tin completely and insert it into the bigger tin. Give it a firm pat to secure it. To check, lift up the shaker, holding it by the smaller tin (don't lift it very high). It should stay secure.

Grip the base of the shaker with one hand and the top with another, using your hand to hold it firmly in place. Shake vigorously, keeping it mostly upright—at a 45-degree angle is good—and pointed away from guests and your sofa. Shake for 15–30 seconds.

Put the shaker down and unseal by wiggling the smaller tin until it comes loose. If it's very tight, grip hold of the larger tin and give it a firm tap just underneath the point where the two tins meet. This should loosen them. Lift off the top tin and strain your drink into a glass, using a strainer.

DRY & REVERSE DRY SHAKING

When making a cocktail with egg white, aquafaba, and sometimes also cream, you will want to either dry shake or reverse dry shake the drink. Dry shaking is shaking all the ingredients without ice, then adding ice and shaking again. Reverse dry shaking is shaking all your ingredients with ice, then straining them out and discarding the ice before shaking the mix again.

The theory with dry shaking is that shaking a cocktail without ice first, and therefore at a higher temperature, allows the drink to emulsify more. The cocktail is better aerated, creating a thicker foam. And it's true, dry shaking does make for a fluffier cocktail, but not as much as reverse dry shaking, which creates a really lovely layer of thick, white foam on top of cocktails.

I alternate between preferring dry and reverse dry shaking. Currently, I think I like dry shaking cocktails with cream and reverse dry shaking cocktails with egg white or aquafaba. This creates lively, velvety-textured cream cocktails and downy-topped egg-white cocktails.

One thing to make sure you always do if you're shaking cocktails with egg white or aquafaba is to fine-strain them. This will catch any curdled bits of protein and give you a smoother drink.

HOW TO STIR

If you can, chill the mixing glass in your refrigerator before using it. Add your drink ingredients to the glass, then fill it two-thirds with ice.

Hold your bar spoon between your thumb and the top two fingers of your dominant hand, then slide the stem in between your middle and ring finger so that the top of your ring finger and your little finger rest against the spoon. Place the back of the spoon against the side of the mixing glass and slide it down until the spoon is almost at the bottom. Gently start to swirl the spoon around the glass, keeping your arm still and using your fingers and wrist to move the spoon. If you imagine using your top two fingers to pull the spoon toward you and then your bottom fingers to push it away, you should start to get the movement. It should be a gentle, elegant motion that makes the ice whisper in the glass.

Usually, you'll stir for 30–45 seconds or around 50–60 revolutions. A shorter stir results in a stronger drink, while a longer stir provides more dilution.

Fit a strainer over your mixing glass and strain your drink into your serving glass.

CAN I REUSE ICE AFTER SHAKING AND STIRRING?

Short answer: no. The ice is spent after one use and should be discarded. The size and wetness of the ice will affect the dilution of your drink. Once ice has been used, it will have broken down into smaller pieces and it'll be wet, which means the second drink you make will be more diluted than the first. Use ice cubes fresh from the freezer which haven't started to melt for shaking drinks.

HOW TO STRAIN

If you're using a cobbler shaker, you can usually strain your drink

using the in-built strainer. But if the cocktail has herbs or chunks of fruit in it, they may block the strainer. In that case, use a Hawthorne strainer.

To use a Hawthorne strainer, remove the lid from a cobbler shaker, French shaker, or the small tin from a Boston shaker. Insert the strainer into the tin so the spring fits snugly around the edge. Turn it so the handle is facing you, then place a finger either side of the handle, holding the strainer in place, and use the rest of your hand to grip the shaker. Pick it up and strain the drink into your glass.

To use a Julep strainer with a mixing glass, insert it into the glass at a 45-degree angle so the bowl is cupping the ice. Place a finger on either side of the handle, holding the strainer in place, and use the rest of your hand to grip the glass. Pick it up and strain the drink into your serving glass.

If you want to fine-strain a cocktail, fit your strainer to your shaker/glass and pick it up with your dominant hand. Hold a small sieve in your nondominant hand and pour the drink through the sieve into your glass.

HOW TO CREATE LAYERS

A layered drink, whether it's a shooter or an extravagant punch, is always going to wow. It's not as hard to do as you think, but it does take a steady hand and a little practice.

The first thing to remember is that all of the technique's success resides in the density of the liquids you're using. Drinks that are high in sugar and low in alcohol tend to be heavy and will sink in the glass. Syrups, like grenadine, will pool at the bottom of the glass; the Tequila Sunrise is a classic example of this (page 24). Sweet liqueurs are next, although cream liqueurs usually float. Fruit juices will also float above syrups. Spirits are normally the lightest ingredients in a float, although cream stays true to the saying and rises to the top.

The temperature of your ingredients will also have an impact, and different brands of the same spirit or liqueur will have a different proof, which will affect their density. Unless you want to get very mad scientist about it, the best thing to do is to settle on your preferred brands, start with your drinks at roughly the same temperature, and remember that the higher the proof, the lighter the drink.

A European bar spoon with the flat disk at the end of the stem is your best friend when it comes to layering. Pour your densest drink into the glass, then turn your bar spoon upside down and hold it in the glass so the flat disk is very close to the surface of the liquid. Slowly pour the next liquid down the length of the bar spoon—it will flow down the spiral of the bar spoon and trickle into the drink, creating a separate layer. Repeat until you have finished your layers.

If you don't have a European bar spoon, pour your first ingredient into your glass then hold your bar spoon (or teaspoon, or soup spoon, depending on the size of the drink) in the glass at a 45-degree angle so the bowl of the spoon is facing upright, touching the side of the glass and just touching the surface of the liquid. Gently pour the drink into the glass. The bowl of the spoon should disperse the drink, so it forms a layer. Repeat as needed.

GARNISHES

Gorgeous Garnishes

They can seem extravagant and a bit extra, but a good garnish can really elevate a drink. Not only do they make your cocktail look spectacular, they often add a layer of aroma that heightens the flavor of your drink.

EASY FREEZES

One quick way to add interest, color, and flavor to your cocktail is by making flavored ice cubes, freezing edible flowers or berries in ice cubes, or simply freezing berries and slices of citrus fruit. Use complementary flavors for the cocktail you're making, such as espresso ice cubes for a White Russian, or adding juniper berries and coriander seed to ice cubes for a Gin & Tonic. Be careful to only use edible ingredients in your ice cubes, especially if you're freezing flowers. Never put anything in a glass that people can't safely consume.

READY-MADE GARNISHES

Cocktail umbrellas, colorful cocktail picks, and reusable straws are a quick way to add color and glam to your mixed drink. Cocktail umbrellas deserve a comeback. Who isn't cheered up by a mini paper umbrella tucked into their drink?

Cocktail picks are essential for spearing maraschino cherries or olives. You can buy them in all sorts of materials, colors, shapes, and sizes. Nothing will cheer up your bar cart more than a pot of multicolored cocktail picks.

Reusable straws are a must if you're making long drinks on the regular. Such a wide variety of straws are available nowadays that the possibilities are endless. Stainless-steel straws are chic, while bamboo can look really good in punches and Tiki drinks. For a bit of fun, multicolored reusable plastic straws will brighten up your drinks again and again.

CITRUS TWISTS

Lots of cocktails are simply garnished with a lemon, lime, or orange twist. If you have a canele cutter or channel knife, then you're on easy street. Pull it along the skin of your citrus fruit and it will create a long, thin ribbon of zest that's perfect for twisting.

If you don't have a garnishing tool, there are two other ways to make a twist. The first is to cut a round slice from your citrus fruit, then cut a notch in it. Run your knife around the fruit pulp to cut it away from the peel. You should be able to open the zest up into a strip. Run the flat of your knife down the zest to slice away any thick layers of the bitter white pith. You should be able to see the pores of the peel through any remaining pith. If not, it's too thick, so carefully slice more away.

Alternatively, use a vegetable peeler to peel a strip of zest off the fruit, then slice off any thick bits of pith. Use your knife to trim the edges to make it look neater. Strips of zest cut this way tend to be thicker and less flexible, so they're not as good for twists. They are good for expressing and then dropping into a glass (see page 15).

To shape your ribbon of citrus zest into a twist, you

can simply twist it or, for something more precise, wrap the peel around a chopstick to create a spiral shape. Slide it off the chopstick and the zest should hold its shape.

If you want to make lots of twists ahead of a party, shape them around a chopstick, then drop them into a bowl of iced water. They should keep their shape and will be ready to use for a couple of hours.

HOW TO EXPRESS A TWIST

When you express a twist you're extracting the citrus oils from the twist of zest. These will add aroma to your cocktail. It's a technique and garnish used a lot with Martinis and other cocktails served with a citrus twist, like a Cosmopolitan.

First of all, if your fruit has been waxed, make sure that has all been washed off. Then peel a strip of zest off the fruit and slice away as much pith as possible. Use your thumbs and forefingers to hold the zest over your finished drink, skin-side down, then gently twist. An almost-invisible mist of citrus oil will spray over the surface of the drink.

Rub the skin of your twist around the rim of your glass to coat it in citrus oil, then drop the twist into your glass. Or discard it and garnish the drink with a fresh twist (I normally drop it in. Waste not, want not).

CITRUS WHEELS, SLICES & WEDGES

A slice of citrus is a very simple garnish that adds a pop of color, plus that all-important extra layer of zingy aroma. A wheel is a round slice of citrus fruit, a slice is half a wheel, and a wedge is a thick chunk of citrus.

When you're cutting wheels and slices, use a sharp paring knife to cut slices around ¼ inch thick. With wheels, make an incision halfway into the round to make it easier to bend the citrus around the glass. For slices, just cut your wheel in half.

To make a wedge, cut your fruit in half then cut each half into quarters lengthwise. Larger fruits, like grapefruits or big oranges, can be cut into six or eight wedges.

HOW TO SALT OR SUGAR RIM A GLASS

Is a Margarita without a salt rim really a Margarita? I have my doubts. Rimming a glass with salt, sugar, a mix of both, or other ingredients like grated chocolate, sprinkles, or Tajin seasoning looks attractive and adds flavor.

Rimming a glass is very simple. You just need to moisten the glass with a liquid, then dip and turn it in your chosen coating. Citrus juice is often used, but you can also use things like sugar syrup, egg white, honey, other fruit juices, or salted caramel.

If you're rimming a glass with salt, use flaky sea salt or kosher salt. Don't use ordinary table salt as this can clump together creating a really thick rim that's unpleasant to drink through.

If you're using a lemon or lime wedge to wet your glass, cut a small slice in the flesh then run that slice along the edge of your glass to coat it in juice. Otherwise, pour your liquid into a saucer and dip your glass in it.

Have your coating ingredient in a separate saucer. Dip the glass in it briefly to coat. You can also hold your glass at a 45-degree angle and turn it to coat the outside edges. This is a handy way to do it if you only want to coat half the glass.

Once your glass has its rim, put it to one side for a few minutes to let it set. If you can, set the glass aside in the refrigerator. This will start to chill it, ready for your drink.

GLASSWARE

Peace, Love & Glassware

Yes, you can serve your cocktails in mason jars and whatever wine glasses you have lying around. But we're disco, not punk, which means we're fabulous, so I'd rather you mixed your Martini in a pitcher and served it in a martini glass than stirred it in a vintage crystal mixing glass but drank it out of a plastic cup.

This may count as putting style over substance, but drinking a cocktail should feel special. This isn't an everyday event, and a Negroni served in a mug feels less like a glamorous treat and more like a cry for help.

However, you don't have to spend a fortune on glasses. Thrift stores can be a good source of beautiful second-hand glasses, as can online marketplaces such as eBay and Etsy. You can also find good-value glasses in lots of grocery and homewares stores. The key thing is to identify what type of cocktail you're most likely to drink often, then buy the shape of glass that matches that. You don't need to own every style of glass out there, just the ones you'll use the most.

HIGHBALL & COLLINS GLASSES

If you like long drinks, such as Tequila Sunrises (page 24), Woo Woos (page 115) and Diet Cokagnes (page 91), then tall glasses are for you.

Highballs are tall, skinny glasses, while collins glasses are tall and fat. The difference is slight, with highballs usually clocking in at 8½–12 ounces and collins glasses measuring 12–16 ounces. So a 12 ounce glass is a safe bet and will cover you for most long drinks, and even some Tiki cocktails if you don't want to invest in hurricane glasses.

ROCKS GLASSES

Fans of Amaretto Sours (page 59), Negronis (page 88), and White Russians (page 63) will want to invest in lowball tumblers. These come in two basic sizes: single rock and double rock (aka the old fashioned glass). Single rock glasses are around 8¾–10 ounces and will comfortably fit a chunk of ice and your drink. They're great for serving single shots neat, and smaller mixed drinks.

Double rock glasses are 10½–12 ounces and they make great midsize glasses for drinks with crushed ice, like Margaritas (page 80) and Stingers (page 64), as well as drinks you want to build in the glass, like a Negroni.

COUPE AND MARTINI GLASSES

If you like your drink served up (without ice), then you need a stemmed cocktail glass to protect your perfectly chilled drink from the warmth of your hands.

Coupes, or champagne saucers, are stemmed glasses with wide bowls. They normally hold around 6 ounces and are the best choice for shaken cocktails. The wide surface area lets the cocktail breathe, and you can inhale the drink's scent as you sip.

Sitting halfway between a coupe and a martini glass, Nick & Nora glasses are bell-shaped and elegant, evoking a kind of speakeasy glamour. They're smaller than coupes, at around 4–5 ounces so they're great for silky, stirred drinks, like a Vodkatini (page 67).

Don't discount the classic v-shaped martini glass, though. You can buy them in 4 ounces, 6 ounces, and 8¾ ounces. While I find the bigger glasses to be a little too bucket-like, the smaller glasses are perfect for Martinis (of course), and I can't imagine drinking a Cosmopolitan (page 75) out of anything else.

WINE, BEER & COPA GLASSES

Spritz lovers will want to ensure they have either wine or copa glasses in their cocktail cabinet.

Copa de Balon glasses are gin and tonic glasses that evolved from red wine glasses in Spain. Their curved shape traps the gin's aroma, while still letting it breathe, and leaves plenty of space for interesting garnishes. They've become the go-to glass for Aperol Spritzes (page 79), but a red wine glass with a wide bowl is just as good.

It goes without saying that if you like Champagne cocktails, then you'll need flute glasses. Flute glasses normally hold around 6 ounces and the shape of the glass is meant to keep the bubbles fizzing. Coupes, by contrast, expose the surface of the drink to more air, which opens up the flavor. If you want a better flow of bubbles, go for a flute.

Beer and beer cocktails can be served in collins or old fashioned glasses, but the sexy curves of a schooner can be hard to resist.

Schooners hold between 14¾ and 16½ ounces, depending on where you are in the world, and have nipped-in bases that flare out before narrowing again at the top. They're a good choice for a regular beer or refreshing beer cocktail, as are flared Pilsner glasses, which come in a range of sizes.

Stemmed, tulip-shaped beer glasses are smaller, holding 13¼ ounces, with a similar, curvy shape. Because they're smaller they're good for strong beers and punchier drinks,

and the stem means you won't hold the glass and warm the drink up.

HURRICANE, SLING & SHOT GLASSES

This is the section of the cocktail cabinet beloved by cocktail aficionados. These glasses are the ones you want when you have your heart set on making a very particular type of drink.

The hurricane glass is big, usually clocking in at 21 ounces. It's named for hurricane lamps and is said to have been developed in New Orleans in the 1940s. It's the go-to glass for Tiki drinks and rum punches, like the Blue Hawaiian (page 68) and Piña Colada (page 103).

Long, tall, and elegant, sling glasses look like highballs that have been on the rack. They're normally narrower at the base, with a flared rim, and measure 11½ ounces. They're the perfect glass for Singapore Slings (page 27) and Long Island Iced Teas (page 116), but you can swap in highballs, collins, or Pilsner glasses if buying sling glasses is a step too far.

Many of us will associate stubby little shot glasses with our college days, but they can be a handy glass to have around. A standard shot glass holds 1–1½ ounces and you'll need them if you want to serve a tray of shooters, like Lemon Drops (page 119), or if you're making Pornstar Martinis (page 83).

Shot glasses are a glass you should be a bit choosy over. Cheap, plain shot glasses will look like you stole them from a bar or haven't given up your college drinking habits, so spend time finding a set that has style, heft, and elegance.

SENSATIONAL SYRUPS

Gimme Some Sugar

Sugar has a bad rep, but when it comes to cocktails, adding sugar is like adding salt when you're cooking. A little sugar enhances the drink's flavor and brings all the ingredients together. It makes the drink smoother, taking the heat out of spirits, enhancing the juiciness of any fruit you've added, and generally just making everything taste better. Use it sparingly and your cocktails will always benefit.

SIMPLE SYRUPS

Simple Syrups are liquid sweeteners that are made by boiling sugar and water together. They disperse sweetness evenly through drinks, ensuring your drinks end up evenly flavored.

The most basic syrup is made with white sugar, but you can experiment by using different sugars such as Demerara or palm sugar for a richer, fudgier flavor. Swapping the sugar for honey will give you a lighter, more floral flavor, while infusing the syrup with herbs and spices is an easy way to add flavors to your mixed drinks.

Simple Syrup

Makes approximately 16 ounces
8¾ ounces sugar
8¾ ounces water

Tip the sugar into a saucepan and pour in the water. Set the pan on medium-high heat and bring to a boil, without stirring. Once the pan is boiling, set your timer for 2 minutes. After 2 minutes, take the pan off the heat and let cool. Transfer to a sterilized jar or tub, seal, then store in the refrigerator for up to 1 month.

Demerara Syrup

Makes approximately 16 ounces
8¾ ounces Demerara sugar
8¾ ounces water

Tip the sugar into a saucepan and pour in the water. Set the pan on medium-high heat and bring to a boil, without stirring. Once the pan is

boiling, set your timer for 2 minutes. After 2 minutes, take the pan off the heat and let cool. Transfer to a sterilized jar or tub, seal, then store in the refrigerator for up to 1 month.

Honey Syrup

Makes approximately 16 ounces

8¾ ounces water
8¾ ounces honey

Pour the water and honey into a pan and set it on medium-high heat. Bring to a boil, without stirring. Once the pan is boiling, set your timer for 2 minutes. After 2 minutes, take the pan off the heat and let cool in the pan. Transfer the syrup to a sterilized jar or tub, seal, then store in the refrigerator for up to 1 month.

FLAVOR VARIATIONS

These infusions all follow the same method: make your Simple Syrup following the basic recipe, then take the pan off the heat. Add the flavoring and let the syrup steep for the suggested time, then strain through a fine-mesh sieve and store in a jar or tub, discarding the flavoring ingredient. They're ready to use straight away. Store them in the refrigerator for up to 1 month.

Vanilla Syrup

Add 1 halved vanilla pod to the syrup and steep for 1–2 hours.

Strain through a sieve into a bowl or pitcher, then transfer to a sterilized jar or bottle.
Used in Angel Wings (page 135)

Chile Syrup

Slice 2 long, red chiles and add them to the syrup. Steep for 20 minutes, then taste to see if it has the right level of heat for you. If you'd like it a little hotter, steep for another 10 minutes. For a milder syrup, don't slice the chiles. Instead, steep them whole in the syrup for 30 minutes to extract the chiles' flavor without the heat.
Used in Holy Mary (page 123) and Spicy Margarita (page 80)

STERILIZING JARS AND BOTTLES

To sterilize glass jars and bottles, preheat your oven to 320°F/160°C. Wash the jars and/or bottles in hot, soapy water (including the lids for the jars, if they have them), then rinse and place on a sheet pan. Slide into the oven and heat for around 15 minutes. Take them out of the oven and let them cool until they're cold enough to handle, then add the syrup and seal.

FLAVORED VODKAS

Drinking the Rainbow

When I was a college student, candy flavored vodkas were all the rage. There was a pub in London that had a whole wall of them. You could drink jelly baby vodka, cola cube vodka, gummy bear vodka, toffee vodka—if it could be found in the confectionery aisle of the local grocery store, then they'd turn it into vodka.

These vodkas were fun. They were brightly colored, full of flavor, and a favorite on celebratory nights out. Obviously, we all need to drink responsibly and no one should be doing shot after shot of vodka but, as a welcome drink for a party, a tray full of ice-cold, neon-hued, flavored vodkas has impact.

For the full rainbow effect, make a batch of Skittles Vodka. Dividing the Skittles up into the different colors means you get five shockingly bright vodkas, each with a subtly different flavor.

SKITTLES VODKA
Makes 5 8-ounce bottles
8¾ ounces Skittles
5 cups (40 ounces) vodka
Simple Syrup (optional, see page 19)

Sterilize five 10-ounce jars. Separate the Skittles into the different colors—you should have a pile of red, green, orange, yellow, and purple. You want around 1¾ ounces of each color.

Add the Skittles to the jars, keeping the colors separate. Top up each jar with 8 to 9 ounces vodka. Seal and give the jars a good shake. Set aside somewhere dry and dark for 24 hours. The Skittles should have all dissolved. If not, give the jars another shake and leave for a further 24 hours.

Sterilize five 8 to 9 ounce bottles. Line a sieve with a muslin cloth and strain the first vodka into a pitcher or bowl. The muslin will catch any bits of undissolved sugar shell. Taste the vodka and add a little Simple Syrup, if you think it needs it—1–2 tablespoons will probably be enough. The different colors will all taste different, so some may need a splash of Simple Syrup and some won't. Pour into a sterilized bottle.

Repeat this with the rest of the vodkas until you have five brightly colored drinks. Seal and store in the refrigerator for up to 1 week, or in the freezer for up to 2 weeks. The colors will begin to fade if kept any longer.

Candy Shop Swaps

You can use this recipe to make similarly brightly colored vodkas with colorful flavored candies like Starbursts, Jolly Ranchers, and jelly beans. Just make sure you separate out the colors, otherwise you'll end up with a very muddy-looking drink.

A smoother alternative to these fruit-candy vodkas is Butterscotch Vodka. This is made with hard butter candies, like Werther's Original, and has a creamy flavor with a rich mouthfeel. This vodka is a good dessert option and would be delicious served alongside shots of espresso.

BUTTERSCOTCH VODKA
Makes 3 cups (24 ounces)
8¾ ounces hard butterscotch candies
17½ ounces vodka
Simple Syrup (optional, see page 19)

Sterilize a 24-ounce jar. Add the butterscotch to the jar and pour over the vodka. Seal and give it a shake. Set aside somewhere dark and dry for 3–4 days, shaking the jar once a day. When the candies have dissolved, the vodka is ready.

Taste and add a little Simple Syrup, if you think it needs it. You can leave the vodka in the jar or pour it into a sterilized bottle. Seal and store in the refrigerator for up to 1 month, or in the freezer for up to 3 months.

USING GOOD BOOZE
Whatever you do, don't use really cheap vodka to make these infusions. The roughness and the heat of the alcohol will fight against the flavors and create something that tastes like cough syrup. You don't have to use a premium vodka; a solid, midpriced bottle that you wouldn't mind drinking with a splash of tonic is perfect.

The Recipes

Note: All recipes are single serve unless otherwise stated.

TEQUILA SUNRISE

On a hot night in June 1972, a barman refused to make Mick Jagger a Margarita. The Rolling Stones had just landed in California and their manager had organized a private party for them at The Trident, a bar in Sausalito. The bar had just installed a new juicer and the bartender, Bobby Lozoff, was keen on experimenting. So when Jagger asked for a Margarita, Lozoff told him he had something better. He whipped up a Tequila Sunrise, a Margarita lengthened with fresh orange juice and stained red with grenadine syrup. Jagger loved it and ordered a round. Then another, and then another. They drank Tequila Sunrises all night. The band took the recipe for the drink with them on tour, and the press was full of reports of the Stones and this hot new cocktail. Within a year, every bar and club in America had Tequila Sunrise on the menu. It's a juicy and refreshing drink that's easy to mix. When you make it at home, use a good-quality tequila—you'll taste it in every sip.

Ingredients

¼ ounce grenadine syrup
¼ ounce crème de cassis
1½ ounces silver tequila
¾ ounce Cointreau
½ ounce fresh lime juice
2½ ounces fresh
    orange juice
Orange wheel and
    maraschino cherry,
    to garnish

Instructions

Pour the grenadine and crème de cassis into a collins glass and gently stir to mix, then top the glass with ice. Pour the tequila, Cointreau, lime juice, and orange juice into a cocktail shaker. Half-fill with ice, seal, and shake well until frosty. Strain the orange mix into the glass. It will float on top of the grenadine layer. Give the drink a gentle stir to encourage the grenadine to bleed upwards into the orange juice. Garnish with an orange wheel and a maraschino cherry. Serve.

Refreshing   Citrus   Sharp

SINGAPORE SLING

Ngiam Tong Boon, the bartender at Raffles Hotel, invented the Singapore Sling in the 1900s. Ngiam ran the Long Bar, a luxurious spot where gentlemen would gather to drink whisky and trade stories. At the time it was socially unacceptable for ladies to drink alcohol in public; they were restricted to modest teas and fruit juices. Ngiam, spotting an opportunity, concocted a Gin Sling that had a rosy glow and a fresh pineapple scent. It looked like a harmless glass of fruit juice, but, obvious only to the bartender and drinker, the drink was laden with booze. The women could get their drink on without anybody realizing, and the bar was soon as popular with women as it was with men. Don't be too shy with the garnishes for this drink. A pineapple wedge is essential, but you can add lemon slices, maraschino cherries, umbrellas, straws, edible flowers . . . whatever takes your fancy. Make it beautiful, then raise a glass to the men and women who know how to party, even when it's forbidden.

Ingredients
4¼ ounces fresh
     pineapple juice
1 ounce London dry gin
½ ounce Heering
     Cherry Liqueur
½ ounce fresh lime juice
¼ ounce grenadine syrup
¼ ounce Cointreau
¼ ounce Bénédictine
     D.O.M. Liqueur
A dash of Angostura bitters
Pineapple wedge and
     edible flower, to garnish

Instructions
Pour all the ingredients into a cocktail shaker, then half-fill it with ice, seal, and shake vigorously to chill.

Fill a tall sling, hurricane, or tulip glass with ice and strain in the cocktail. Garnish with a wedge of pineapple, an edible flower, and whatever else your imagination runs to.

Tropical   Tangy   Boozy

SEX ON THE BEACH

This is one of those deceptively easy-to-drink cocktails that can lead to trouble if you're not wise with your measurements. The sweet combination of fruit juices masks the booze, so it seems more innocent than it is. But this fruity cocktail packs a punch and I suspect it got its name because of what happens after you've drunk a couple of these as much as it reflects the two-tone nature of the drink (the sex part is the scarlet pool of cranberry-vodka, while the beach is the peach schnapps-infused layer of orange juice). I've actually dialed down the booze in this version of the drink, and added a splash of lime juice to sharpen up the citrus. It's a crisp, well-balanced mix of sweet and sour that could easily be turned into a pitcher drink. Simply pour as many equal measurements as you need into a pitcher full of ice and stir until it's chilled. If you do want to put a bit of heat back into the drink, up the vodka to 1½ ounces.

Ingredients

¾ ounce vodka

1½ ounces cranberry juice

½ ounce Chambord

¾ ounce peach schnapps

1½ ounces fresh orange juice

½ ounce fresh lime juice

Orange wheel, maraschino cherry, and mint sprig, to garnish

Instructions

Pour the vodka, cranberry juice, and Chambord into a cocktail shaker. Half-fill with ice, seal, and shake to chill. Fill a hurricane glass with ice and strain in the cranberry-vodka mix.

Tip the ice out of the shaker, rinse it clean, then add the schnapps, orange juice, and lime juice. Half-fill with fresh ice, seal, and shake. Strain the orange-schnapps mix into the cranberry-vodka mix, pouring close to the ice. The orange mix will slowly blend with the cranberry, eventually pooling underneath it.

Cut a slice in an orange wheel to open it out, then spear it on a cocktail pick with a cherry and tuck it in the glass. Add a mint sprig and serve with a reusable straw to stir the drink.

Crisp

 Fruity

 Boozy

MIDORI SOUR

Midori is the ultimate disco drink. It was launched in America in 1978 with a party at Studio 54, the infamous New York nightclub. The stars of *Saturday Night Fever* were invited to give the event some much-needed disco glamour. After the shindig, Midori-based cocktails were the hottest drinks in town. Even without John Travolta raising a glass, Midori is pretty disco. It has an ultra-bright, neon-green color and a sweet, fruity flavor that's similar to pear drops. It gets its flavor and light, syrupy taste from musk melons—orange-hued melons that have a delicate, sherbet-like flesh. Midori is at its best when balanced with a splash of citrus, so using it in a sour is a no-brainer. This cocktail is lengthened with a splash of soda water. Use as much soda as you like, depending on how refreshing you want to make the drink.

Ingredients

1 ounce vodka

1 ounce Midori liqueur

½ ounce fresh lemon juice

½ ounce fresh lime juice

Soda water, to top up

Maraschino cherry,
   to garnish

Instructions

Pour the vodka, Midori, lemon juice, and lime juice into a cocktail shaker. Half-fill with ice, seal, and shake well until chilled.

Fill an old fashioned glass with ice and strain in the cocktail mix. Top up with a splash of soda water, gently stir to mix, and serve garnished with a maraschino cherry.

Fruity   Bright   Sherbet

SLOE COMFORTABLE SCREW

Orange juice was the most popular mixer in the 1970s, and one of the easiest ways to invent a drink was to take a spirit and then simply add O.J. Give the cocktail a saucy name and you were guaranteed a hit. The Sloe Comfortable Screw is part of the Screwdriver family of drinks, a classic spirit-and-orange-juice mix that has at least half a dozen variations. You can enjoy your Screw sloe, hard, with a kiss, a bang, against a wall, or in between the sheets—whatever your tastes run to. I like the Sloe Comfortable Screw version for the swirl of ruby red sloe gin that gives the orange juice a modest blush, and for the smoke and spice combo of bourbon and Southern Comfort. They partner up beautifully with the tangy citrus, creating a smoothly refreshing drink that should be one of the brunch greats. Serve with plenty of ice in a roomy glass with a reusable straw.

Ingredients

1½ ounces Southern Comfort

¾ ounce bourbon

4¼ ounces fresh orange juice

½ ounce sloe gin

Instructions

Pour the Southern Comfort, bourbon, and orange juice into a mixing glass, then half-fill it with ice. Stir for 30–45 seconds to chill (I count 50 revolutions of the spoon while I'm stirring).

Fill a collins glass with ice and strain in the cocktail. Trickle the sloe gin into the glass, then serve straight away with a reusable straw.

Tangy   Smoky   Smooth

BRANDY ALEXANDER

Originally known as Alexander #2, this luxurious after-dinner drink is a perfect example of the decadent, cream-based cocktails that were popular during the disco era. The Brandy Alexander has actually been around since the 1930s and was a riff on the Gin Alexander, or the Alexander #1. It's an indulgent combination of brandy, chocolate, and cream. With ingredients like that, it's no surprise it managed to stay on bar menus when other dessert drinks faded away. The drink's toffee flavors are complemented by a final dusting of nutmeg, which adds a warming touch of spice. I think this dash of sweet spice is essential, but if you don't like nutmeg, try swapping in a pinch of ground cinnamon or cardamom. Reverse shaking the cocktail helps give it a silkily smooth texture. If you want it to be extra velvety, add ½ ounce fresh egg white or aquafaba and reverse dry shake (see page 11 for a guide on dry and reverse dry shaking).

Ingredients

1½ ounces cognac

1 ounce dark crème de cacao

1 ounce light cream

Freshly grated nutmeg, to garnish

Instructions

Place a Nick & Nora glass or a small coupe in the freezer for 10 minutes, fill with ice, and set aside to chill.

Pour the cognac, dark crème de cacao, and light cream into a shaker, seal, and shake for around 30 seconds until it feels and sounds light.

Add a generous amount of ice to the shaker, seal, and shake again. Fine-strain into the chilled glass, discarding any ice, and serve dusted with a little freshly grated nutmeg.

Indulgent/Luxurious   Silky

DIRTY MARTINI

If there's one cocktail that never goes out of fashion, it's the Martini. A sophisticated drink—in the most disreputable way—an ice-cold Martini is guaranteed to give any occasion a gloss of glamour. This "dirty" version is made with a teaspoonful of brine from a jar of green olives. The brine adds a salty tang to the mix, and gives the drink a little murk. A classic gin Martini is as crystal clear as the Arctic Ocean. Add a splash of brine and it becomes hazy, as if a smoky swirl of fog has flowed into the glass. When you're stirring your drink, make sure it is brine that you're adding to your Martini. Some olives are jarred in oil and stirring that into your Martini will create an unappetizing slick on top of your drink. Also make sure you're using a good-quality gin. It doesn't have to be a London dry gin—your favorite craft gin or Old Tom will also make a good Martini. Ideally, you want a gin that isn't packed with botanicals, as these can fight in the glass with the olive brine's savoriness. And if you're using good gin, then also use the best French vermouth you can afford. Never skimp on a Martini—and never drink more than two.

Ingredients

¼ ounce dry French
  vermouth

2 ounces good-quality gin

¼ ounce brine from a
  jar of green olives

Green olives, to garnish

Instructions

Put your martini glass into the freezer for at least 30 minutes, or fill it with ice.

Half-fill a mixing glass with ice and pour in the vermouth. Stir a few times to coat the ice. Pour in the gin and add the olive brine. Stir for 30 seconds or 50 revolutions of the spoon, then fine-strain the Martini into your glass.

You can drop an olive straight into the glass or spear a couple on a pick and lay it in the glass.

Crisp   Dry   Boozy

SNOWBALL

There was a time when the Snowball was one of the most popular mixed drinks in Great Britain. In the 1970s, drinking a Snowball was a shortcut to a more glamorous world, one that was filled with frothy cocktails, bright flavors, and cosmopolitan liqueurs. Some of the Snowball's decline can be attributed to sloppy mixing, when pubs just dumped Advocaat and lemonade in a glass without including a good squeeze of fresh lime juice—an essential ingredient for cutting through the liqueur's creaminess. It's also partly down to a squeamish horror of a liqueur that's made with eggs. But if you think of Advocaat as a kind of boozy custard, then it becomes much more enjoyable to drink. The Snowball is a great party drink. It's quick and easy to make, and tastes like a grown-up cream soda. If you're looking for a fresh drink to have while you get ready to go out, try a Snowball and see how much more fabulous it makes you feel.

Ingredients

½ ounce fresh lime juice

1½ ounces Advocaat

3½ ounces sparkling lemonade

Maraschino cherries, to garnish

Instructions

Fill a highball glass with ice. Pour in the lime juice and Advocaat, then pour in the lemonade, gently stirring as you add it so the drink develops a light froth on top (the snow in your Snowball).

Thread maraschino cherries onto a cocktail pick and rest it on the rim of the glass to garnish.

Crisp   Indulgent/Luxurious   Creamy

PINK SQUIRREL

It's time to bring back the dessert cocktail. Cute and creamy, these dinky drinks are a deliciously indulgent way to cap off a meal. They're a great alternative to an actual dessert, or you can pair them with a matching sweet. This pale-pink drink tastes like strawberry shortcake, so it would be good combined with any berry-based treat. I can imagine it being served alongside a slice of strawberry cheesecake, or a scoop of raspberry ripple ice cream. It gets its pink color from crème de noyaux, a French liqueur that's made from apricot/peach stones and cherry pits. Crème de noyaux has a rich, marzipan flavor and gets its rosy-red color from cochineal. It dropped out of fashion and would have vanished entirely if it wasn't for Tempus Fugit Spirits, a liquor company dedicated to recreating forgotten nineteenth-century spirits and liqueurs. In 2013, after many years of research and testing, they brought out their version of crème de noyaux. If you can't find crème de noyaux in your local wine store, you can swap in amaretto or Frangelico. The magic of this drink lies in combining a syrupy, nutty liqueur with a dash of chocolate and a splash of cream. Don't skip the nutmeg, which gives an aromatic lift at the end. Alternatively, rose petals and red peppercorns make a decadent garnish.

Ingredients

¾ ounce crème de noyaux

¾ ounce white crème de cacao

2 ounces heavy cream

Freshly grated nutmeg, to garnish

Instructions

To chill, place a Nick & Nora glass or a small coupe in the freezer for 10 minutes, or in the refrigerator for 1 hour (or fill with ice).

Pour the three creams into a shaker. Don't add ice. Seal and dry shake for around 30 seconds or until it feels light and foamy.

Add ice, seal the shaker again, and shake for 15 seconds to chill.

Fine-strain into the chilled glass. To garnish, grate a little nutmeg or garnish with rose petals and red peppercorns

Creamy   Indulgent/Luxurious   Marzipan

HARVEY WALLBANGER

If you love Aperol Spritzes and Negronis then (surprisingly) this long, luscious cocktail could be for you. The reason: Galliano L'Autentico. A honey-colored liqueur from Italy, it's flavored with fistfuls of herbs and spices, including cardamom, sage, thyme, cinnamon, and sandalwood. The top notes are peppermint, anise, and vanilla, which give it a sweetly herbal flavor that fans of more stringent Italian amaros, like Campari, will enjoy. Floated on top of this simple vodka-and-O.J. cocktail, it immediately lifts the drink and gives it a subtle, sophisticated flavor. You can drink the cocktail through the layer of Galliano, or serve your Wallbanger with straws or a swizzle stick to stir it in. If you're wondering why this juice-based cocktail is stirred rather than shaken, against all the normal rules of cocktail making, it's to make sure it doesn't get too diluted. Shaken would make it too wet, while stirring chills the drink without dimming the flavors.

Ingredients

1¼ ounces vodka

3 ounces fresh orange juice

¼ ounce Simple Syrup (page 19)

A few dashes of orange bitters

½ ounce Galliano L'Autentico Liqueur

Orange slice and maraschino cherry, to garnish

Instructions

Pour the vodka, orange juice, and Simple Syrup into a mixing glass. Dash in some orange bitters. Add ice and stir for 30–45 seconds to chill.

Fill a collins glass with ice and strain in the cocktail.

Pour the Galliano down your bar spoon to float it on the top of the drink (there's a how-to guide on page 12 for this technique). Drop in an orange slice and maraschino cherry to garnish.

Herbal   Tangy   Refreshing

GRASSHOPPER

Delightfully fluffy, this dessert cocktail is like drinking melted mint-choc-chip ice cream. It gets its pale-green color from crème de menthe, a sweet liqueur that was developed at the end of the nineteenth century by French pharmacist Émile Giffard. He was investigating the digestive properties of mint and found that people reported feeling much better after a meal if they finished it with a glass of mint-flavored booze. Not long after Giffard's invention, dessert cocktails like the Grasshopper started appearing on bar menus and they stayed popular until the late 1970s, when low-fat diets spoiled our love for creamy after-dinner drinks. You can prepare the glasses ahead, coating the rims with chocolate, and keep them in the refrigerator. Whizz the ingredients together with a cupful of ice in a blender, then transfer to the refrigerator. Before serving, whizz the mix in the blender to get the fluff back, then pour into the chilled glasses.

Ingredients

¼ ounce Simple Syrup (page 19)

½ tablespoon grated dark chocolate, plus extra to garnish (optional)

1 ounce green crème de menthe

1 ounce white crème de cacao

1½ ounces light cream

Instructions

Pour the Simple Syrup into a saucer. Sprinkle ½ tablespoon of grated chocolate onto a separate saucer. Dip the rim of a coupe or small martini glass in the Simple Syrup, then turn it in the chocolate to coat the rim. Transfer to the refrigerator for at least 10 minutes to set.

Pour the crème de menthe, crème de cacao, and light cream into a cocktail shaker. Half-fill the shaker with ice, seal, and shake well to chill, then strain the mix into a glass (not the coupe). Discard the ice, return the mix to the shaker and shake for around 30 seconds or until the cocktail feels light and foamy in the tin.

Fine-strain into the coupe and garnish with a pinch of grated chocolate, if desired.

● Chocolate   ● Minty

PINK LADY

I'd love to tell you that this cocktail was named after the Pink Ladies in *Grease*, but sadly I can't. This zingy gin cocktail has been popping up on bar menus since the early twentieth century and was probably named after Hazel Dawn, an actress who made her name in *The Pink Lady*—a Broadway smash way back in 1911. It's a chic drink that riffs on a gin sour and gets its deep fuchsia glow from grenadine, a sticky syrup made from pomegranate juice. A slug of applejack gives the cocktail extra heft. Applejack often gets overlooked—bourbon's smooth glamour and rye's down-home appeal have eclipsed it in the world of American spirits—but it deserves a spot in your cocktail cabinet. Applejack and apple brandy are sometimes used interchangeably, but a blended applejack is a mix of neutral spirits and 20% apple brandy. It's a party spirit that's ideal for cocktails because, in the words of Rizzo, it's not "too pure to be pink."

Ingredients

1¼ ounces London dry gin

½ ounce applejack

¾ ounce fresh lemon juice

¾ ounce grenadine

½ ounce fresh egg white or aquafaba

Amarena or maraschino cherries, to garnish

Instructions

Put a coupe glass into the freezer for 10 minutes, or fill it with ice and set aside to chill. Pour all the ingredients into a cocktail shaker, then half-fill it with ice, seal, and shake. Strain the cocktail into a glass (not the chilled coupe) and discard the ice.

Pour the mix back into the shaker, seal, and shake again without ice for around 30 seconds or until it feels light and foamy. Fine-strain the drink into the chilled coupe. Thread cherries onto a cocktail pick and rest it on the rim of the glass to garnish.

 Boozy   Tangy

PARADISE

This juicy gin cocktail falls under the category of Very Wet Martinis, and it's a precursor to the fruit-based Vodka Martinis that swept through bars and clubs in the 1980s and '90s. A Wet Martini is one made with equal quantities of vermouth or other liqueur to gin. The more of the "mixer" spirit there is, the wetter the Martini. The Paradise uses a generous slug of apricot brandy in place of vermouth and, like a lot of disco drinks, it also uses orange juice as a mixer. I've added a teaspoon of lemon juice to balance out the citrus, which gives the cocktail a marmalade flavor that will appeal to fans of Breakfast Martinis. Apricot brandies often include the apricot kernels in the production process, which adds a whisper of almond to the finished drink. If you want to swap out the apricot brandy, try using crème de noyaux. Not only will this give the drink a marzipan finish, it will dye it a pale, blush pink. Amaretto would also be a good sub. You do have to keep the gin, though, and make it a juniper-forward London dry gin to fill your glass with fresh and exhilarating aromatics.

Ingredients

1½ ounces London dry gin
¾ ounce apricot brandy
2 ounces fresh orange juice
¼ ounce fresh lemon juice
A dash of orange bitters
Orange twist, to garnish

Instructions

Put a small coupe or Nick & Nora glass into the freezer for 30 minutes, or fill it with ice and set aside to chill.

Pour the gin, apricot brandy, orange juice, and lemon juice into a cocktail shaker. Dash in some orange bitters, seal, and shake for around 15 seconds to chill. Fine-strain into the chilled glass.

Express an orange twist over the cocktail (see page 15 for a how-to guide to this technique) and rub the rim with the twist, before dropping it into the glass to garnish.

Aromatic   Citrus

GODFATHER

The '70s wasn't just a good decade for disco, dancing, and drinks. It was a golden age for movies too, and Francis Ford Coppola's mafia epic *The Godfather* was the king of the silver screen. When Coppola's mobster movie landed in 1972, it had a huge impact on pop culture. People spoke the slang, cooked the food, and crafted things in tribute to Don Corleone, including the Godfather cocktail. A 2:1 mix of Scottish whisky and amaretto, it was an elegant drink that balanced the robust vanilla oak of whisky with amaretto's syrupy almond notes. In the same way that *The Godfather* spawned *The Godfather Part II* (and another movie we won't talk about), the cocktail led to the creation of the God Damn collection of cocktails. There was the Godmother (vodka and amaretto) and the Godchild (brandy and amaretto), but neither of those had the staying power of the original. My version bumps up the whisky and dials down the amaretto, as well as floating a spoonful of smoky Laphroaig over the top. This gives the drink a hint of wood smoke on the nose, followed by a spirit-forward sip that tastes like power.

Ingredients

2 ounces blended
   Scottish whisky
¾ ounce amaretto
¼ ounce Laphroaig whisky
Orange twist, to garnish

Instructions

Pour the blended whisky and amaretto into a mixing glass. Half-fill it with ice and stir for 30–45 seconds.

Fill an old fashioned glass with ice and strain in the amaretto mix. Pour the Laphroaig down the stem of your bar spoon to float it on the top of the drink (there's a how-to guide on page 12 for this technique).

Serve straight away, garnished with an orange twist.

Smoky   Marzipan

HOT PANTS

What would disco be without hot pants? Satin, sequin-spangled, or, in this case, full of booze, short shorts are perfect for both dancing and drinking. The original Hot Pants cocktail appeared in *Mr. Boston Official Bartender's Guide* in 1974. It was mainly tequila with just a dash of peppermint schnapps and grapefruit juice. I've upped the fresh grapefruit juice in this version to give the cocktail a fruitier profile and take it closer to the traditional ratios for a sour. The result is a minty, easy-to-drink take on a Margarita. The peppermint schnapps is a bit of a wildcard ingredient, but it does give this cocktail an Arctic briskness that makes it seem extra refreshing. I think this would be a perfect summer party drink, especially on hot, humid days when there's no escape from the heat. You could easily size up the ingredients and mix it in pitchers, rather than shaking it, if you're catering for a crowd.

Ingredients

¼ teaspoon granulated sugar

¼ teaspoon flaky sea salt

2 teaspoons Simple Syrup (page 19)

1½ ounces silver tequila

1 ounce fresh grapefruit juice

½ ounce peppermint schnapps

Lime or grapefruit twist or wedge, to garnish

Instructions

Sprinkle the sugar and salt into a saucer and pour 1 teaspoon of Simple Syrup into a separate saucer. Dip the rim of an old fashioned glass in the syrup and then in the sugar and salt mix to lightly coat it. Set aside, ideally in the refrigerator to chill.

Pour the tequila, grapefruit juice, peppermint schnapps, and remaining 1 teaspoon of Simple Syrup into a shaker. Half-fill the tin with ice, seal, and shake well to chill.

Fill the old fashioned glass with ice and strain in the cocktail. Garnish with a lime or grapefruit twist or wedge.

 Refreshing

Citrus

 Minty

JUNGLE BIRD

Jeffrey Ong, the Beverage Manager at the Kuala Lumpur Hilton in Malaysia, invented this Tiki-style rum cocktail in 1973 and it quickly became the hotel's signature welcome drink. Guests would arrive at the Hilton, hot and sweaty from their journey, and would then be shown to the hotel's bar, the Aviary, where they could relax and recuperate over a chilled drink. The Jungle Bird was originally served in a ceramic, bird-shaped cup, which had a spout in the bird's tail that guests could drink from. Over time the hotel shifted to serving the drink in beautifully engraved glasses. So, if you're worried about overgarnishing this drink, don't be. It's impossible to go too far with the garnishes for this cocktail, whether it's a simple pineapple wedge or a glittering jumble of umbrellas, citrus slices, cherries, and swizzle sticks. The drink itself is peachy pink and the Campari, which adds bite, refreshes the tropical sweetness of the pineapple juice.

Ingredients

1½ ounces dark rum

¾ ounce Campari

1½ ounces pineapple juice

¼ ounce fresh lime juice

¼ ounce Demerara Syrup (page 19)

Pineapple wedge and lime wheel, to garnish

Instructions

Pour all the ingredients into a cocktail shaker. Half-fill the shaker with ice, seal, and shake until chilled.

Fill an old fashioned glass with ice and strain in the cocktail mix. Thread fresh pineapple cubes onto a pick and perch on the rim of the glass to garnish. Alternatively, fix a pineapple wedge and lime wheel to the rim.

Serve and enjoy.

 Aromatic

Tropical

 Bitter

GOLDEN CADILLAC

If the idea of a dessert cocktail seems a bit too rich to you, then this straw-colored drink is the after-dinner libation for you. Like most dessert drinks, it's made with a mix of cream, chocolate liqueur, and another spirit—Galliano L'Autentico here. But unlike the others, this one features a splash of orange juice. This half-measure of citrus cuts through the cream, lifting the drink and making it smooth, refreshing, and easy to sip. It tastes like a zesty milkshake and it would make a great brunch cocktail, or a sun-downer on a terrace with a view. In the intro to every cocktail in this book that features nutmeg, I say: "Don't skip the nutmeg." I always mean that, but I really, *really* mean it here. The final dusting of nutmeg is essential, adding an elegant layer of fragrance that elevates this simple, orange pudding of a drink.

Ingredients

1 ounce white crème
    de cacao

1 ounce Galliano
    L'Autentico Liqueur

1 ounce light cream

½ ounce fresh orange juice

A few dashes of
    orange bitters

Freshly grated nutmeg,
    to garnish

Instructions

Put a small coupe or Nick & Nora glass in the freezer for 30 minutes, or fill it with ice and set aside to chill.

Pour the white crème de cacao, Galliano, light cream, and orange juice into a shaker. Dash in a couple of drops of orange bitters. Half-fill the shaker with ice, seal, and shake well until the tin is frosty.

Strain the cocktail into a glass (not the coupe) and discard the ice. Pour the drink back in, seal, and shake again for around 30 seconds, or until the drink feels light and foamy. Fine-strain the cocktail into the chilled glass. Grate over some nutmeg to garnish.

Crisp   Tangy   Citrus

AMARETTO SOUR

The first time I tried amaretto, I drank it from a plastic cup at a sample station in the aisle of a grocery store. It wasn't an auspicious place to try a liqueur for the first time, but I've never forgotten it. I was with my mum and, after the first sip, we both looked at each other and silently agreed to add a bottle of amaretto to our shopping basket. I still think amaretto is one of the most delicious liqueurs ever invented, and the Amaretto Sour is the perfect way to serve it. It's fresh, sharp, and tastes like a lemon meringue pie. The spirit's almond flavor gives the drink an almost biscuity base note, while the combination of lemon and egg white creates a creamy top note of citrus. The cloud-like layer of white foam gives the drink a soft, smooth texture that feels incredibly indulgent. I tried dry shaking, reverse dry shaking, and simply shaking this cocktail to see which method gave the fluffiest foam top, and reverse dry shaking won out. Shaking everything over ice ensures all the ingredients are chilled to the same temperature, then removing the ice lets the drink expand in the shaker. Whether you're looking for a pre-dinner drink, a cocktail to sip while gossiping with your friends, or something to sink into at the end of the night, this is the cocktail for you.

Ingredients

2 ounces amaretto

1 ounce fresh lemon juice

½ ounce fresh egg white or aquafaba

A few dashes of Angostura bitters

Lemon slice and maraschino cherry, to garnish

Instructions

Pour the amaretto, lemon juice, and egg white or aquafaba into a shaker. Dash in some Angostura bitters. Half-fill the tin with ice, seal, and shake for around 15 seconds. Strain out the cocktail into a clean glass and discard the ice.

Return the sour mix to the tin, seal, and shake again until the cocktail feels light and foamy. Fill an old fashioned glass with ice and fine-strain in the Amaretto Sour. Spear a lemon slice and maraschino cherry on a cocktail pick and rest on the glass. Serve straight away.

Marzipan   Refreshing   Indulgent/Luxurious

BETWEEN THE SHEETS

If you have worked your way down the list of disco drinks and been dismayed by how many of them are fruity, syrupy, or laden with cream, then a Between the Sheets is for you. In spite of the saucy-sounding name, this is a sophisticated mixed drink from the early twentieth century and it is as dry as the Sahara in the height of summer. This is a cocktail for grownups who prefer to sip their liquor. I think of this as a drink for wallflowers, and I count myself as one of them. I'm a people watcher, and I enjoy finding a good spot where I can observe the party as it gets going and swap stories with guests as they come and go. Although, after a couple of these strong drinks, I'd probably find myself on the dance floor with everybody else. The traditional ratios are equal quantities of rum, brandy, and Cointreau with a dash of lemon juice for tartness. I've bumped up the lemon juice to keep the cocktail sharp and also help bring out the citrus flavors in the Cointreau.

Ingredients
1 ounce light rum
1 ounce cognac
1 ounce Cointreau
½ ounce fresh lemon juice
Lemon twist, to garnish

Instructions
Put a martini or coupe glass into the freezer for at least 30 minutes, or fill it with ice and set aside to chill.

Pour all the ingredients into a shaker and half-fill with ice. Seal and shake vigorously until chilled. Fine-strain into the chilled glass (discarding any ice from the glass first). Garnish with a lemon twist to serve.

 Dry

 Boozy

 Citrus

WHITE RUSSIAN

Like many cream-based cocktails, the White Russian swaggered its way through the 1970s only to fall from favor when fruit-based cocktails became all the rage in the '80s and '90s. But unlike other creamy cocktails, the White Russian got a second act. It was The Dude's drink of choice in *The Big Lebowski*, the Coen Brothers' cult 1998 movie that gave White Russians, bowling, and stealing rugs a lick of sleazy glamour. It's a very easy cocktail to mix, but you should remember that it is heftily laden with booze. When you mix it, make sure that you use a good-quality vodka, as it makes up half the drink. If the vodka is coarse and rough, you won't end up with the smooth, sippable cocktail that made life manageable for The Dude. You can float the cream on top of the vodka and coffee liqueur, sipping the cocktail through the cream, or serve it with a reusable straw or a swizzle stick to stir the drink together, creating a dangerously strong cocktail that tastes just like coffee ice cream.

Ingredients
2 ounces vodka
1 ounce coffee liqueur
1 ounce light cream

Instructions
Pour the vodka and coffee liqueur into a mixing glass, then half-fill it with ice. Stir for 30–45 seconds to chill. Fill an old fashioned glass with ice and strain in the vodka mix.

Pour the cream down the stem of your bar spoon into the glass (turn to page 12 for a how-to guide to this technique) to float it on top of the drink. Serve straight away.

Indulgent/Luxurious   Creamy   Coffee

STINGER

A zinger of a drink, this minty-fresh cocktail is a cheeky mix of warming cognac and cooling peppermint. Like many cocktails that were popular in the '70s, the Stinger had its first heyday in the 1920s and 1930s when the Vanderbilt family would serve them at high-society parties. The Stinger kept cropping up at bars and parties over the next few decades, and it was popular with fictional drinkers too. James Bond enjoys a Stinger in *Diamonds Are Forever*, while Frank Sinatra and Bing Crosby linger over them in *High Society*. Classically, it's shaken and served up—unusual for an all-spirit cocktail—but more-modern versions of the drink are stirred and served over crushed ice. It's a bracing cocktail that's guaranteed to give you tingles. Serve it at a pool party, or try it after dark on hot, summer nights when you want an exhilarating way to break the heat.

Ingredients

2 ounces cognac

1 ounce white crème de menthe

Mint sprig, to garnish

Instructions

Pour the cognac and white crème de menthe into a mixing glass, then half-fill it with ice. Stir for 30–45 seconds to chill.

Fill an old fashioned glass with crushed ice and strain in the cocktail. Tuck a mint sprig into the glass and serve.

VODKATINI

Vodka: a spirit that goes in and out of fashion as often as jumpsuits and go-go boots. One minute it's cool and chic to drink vodka (and wear jumpsuits), the next it's unbearably unfashionable and no one would be seen dead ordering it. Currently, vodka is in fashion. This is as much to do with people growing bored of drinking artisanal gins as it is down to the quality of vodka finally improving over the past couple years. Well-crafted vodkas that are distilled with an eye to the final flavor and mouthfeel, rather than just the raw heat of the alcohol, have slipped into the marketplace and made the idea of a Vodka Martini interesting once again. Mixed with a really good vodka and a dry, herbal vermouth, a Vodkatini is a slippery, silky drink that chills and warms all at the same time. If you prefer your Martini dirty, swap the lemon twist for ¼ ounce olive brine and follow the method on page 36.

Ingredients

¼ ounce dry French vermouth

2 ounces good-quality vodka

Lemon twist, to garnish

Instructions

Put your martini glass into the freezer for at least 30 minutes, or fill it with ice and set aside to chill.

Half-fill a mixing glass with ice and pour in the vermouth. Stir a few times to coat the ice. Pour in the vodka. Stir for 30 seconds, then fine-strain the Vodkatini into your glass (discarding any ice from the martini glass first).

Express the lemon twist over the Vodkatini (see the how-to guide on page 15 for this technique), then rub the zest around the rim of the glass. Drop the zest into the Vodkatini to garnish, and serve.

Crisp   Dry   Boozy

BLUE HAWAIIAN

As beautifully blue as the Pacific Ocean, this long, beach cocktail is a colorful riff on the Piña Colada. The traditional tropical mix of pineapple and coconut are the key flavors here, and they're sharpened up with a splash of fresh lime juice. The original version of this drink is made with coconut cream, which gives the cocktail a rich flavor and luxurious consistency, but I find it smoother and more refreshing made with coconut milk. The most important ingredient is the blue curaçao. It's an orange-scented liqueur that's named after the Caribbean island of Curaçao where the bitter oranges that flavor the drink grow. I have no idea what possessed someone to start coloring curaçao blue, but one day they did and now there is a range of dazzlingly azure liqueurs on the market. They make the most cheerful drinks, each one as inviting as the sea on a warm, summer's day.

68

Ingredients
1½ ounces light rum
¾ ounce blue curaçao
3 ounces pineapple juice
¾ ounce coconut milk
½ ounce fresh lime juice
Pineapple wedge
  and maraschino
  cherry, to garnish

Instructions
Pour all the ingredients into a cocktail shaker, then half-fill it with ice. Seal and shake until chilled.

Fill a hurricane glass with crushed ice and strain in the cocktail. Spear a pineapple wedge and a maraschino cherry on a cocktail pick and balance them on the glass to garnish. Serve with a reusable straw and cocktail umbrella, if desired, because we are always at home to glamour.

NICE & FREEZY

You can turn this into a frozen cocktail by pouring all the ingredients into a blender, adding 2 cups of ice and blitzing until slushy. This is an easy way to turn the drink into a party pitcher. Just size up the ingredients, add ice and blend.

 Creamy   Tropical   Coconut

MERRY WIDOW FIZZ

Serves 2

Frothy and foamy, Gin Fizzes are one of the most enjoyable types of cocktail to whip up at home. They're normally mixed like a sour, with a measure of something sweet and something sour to add a syrupy tang to a generous measure of booze, but then they're shaken with egg white (or aquafaba—chickpea water—if you prefer your cocktails vegan) and lengthened with soda water. The result is a tall drink with a silky texture and gorgeous two-tone appearance. This '70's fizz is made with sloe gin, which provides both the heat and the sweetness, as well as coloring the drink a pretty shade of pink. A combination of orange and lemon juices ensures the flavors are tart and refreshing. Reverse dry shaking the ingredients will help give your cocktail a really good, creamy layer of white foam, like meringue on top of a pie. Go to page 11 for more information on this cocktail-mixing technique.

Ingredients

2 ounces fresh orange juice

2 ounces fresh lemon juice

2 teaspoons superfine sugar

3 ounces sloe gin

1 ounce fresh egg white or aquafaba

4¼ ounces soda water, chilled

Lemon slices, to garnish

Instructions

Pour the orange and lemon juices into a cocktail shaker and add the sugar. Stir for 1–2 minutes to dissolve the sugar.

Pour in the sloe gin and egg white or aquafaba, then seal and shake until the tin feels light and foamy. Add a generous cupful of ice to the shaker, seal again, then shake until well chilled.

Fill 2 highball glasses with ice and fine-strain in the Merry Widow mix. Top up each glass with chilled soda water. Gently stir to just start to mix, then tuck lemon slices into the glasses to garnish and serve.

Silky   Sweet   Tangy

JAPANESE SLIPPER

Nothing says party like a neon-green Martini. This brightly colored riff on a sour is made with Midori, the Japanese musk melon liqueur that can light up a room from inside the bottle. The drink's name, Midori, is taken from the Japanese word for green. Specifically, it's the shade of green that you find in young leaves and shoots, and the liqueur is dyed a vibrant neon color to match that fresh, invigorating vibe. Midori's fruity melon flavor matches up deliciously with Cointreau's dry citrus notes and the sharp tang of fresh lemon juice. These three ingredients were first put together by Jean-Paul Bourguignon, a French bartender who was working at Mietta's Restaurant in Melbourne. In 1984 Midori's sales reps visited the bar, keen to crack the Aussie cocktail scene after triumphing in Europe and America. Jean-Paul's inspired, candy store-flavored Martini helped them sell Midori to Melbourne's drinking classes and to cocktail connoisseurs around the world. It's a sweetie of a drink that's easy to shake and sip.

Ingredients

1 ounce Cointreau
1 ounce Midori
1 ounce fresh lemon juice
Maraschino cherry,
   to garnish

Instructions

Put a martini glass into the freezer for at least 30 minutes, or fill it with ice and set aside to chill.

Pour all the ingredients into a cocktail shaker and half-fill it with ice. Seal and shake vigorously until chilled. Fine-strain the mix into the chilled glass (discarding any ice from the glass first).

Drop a maraschino cherry into the glass to garnish, and serve.

Fresh   Tangy   Sherbet

COSMOPOLITAN

Any cocktail that appears in *Sex and the City* is disco by me. A long-time favorite of Carrie, Samantha, Miranda, and Charlotte, the Cosmo was the girls' drink of choice in the TV show and they ordered a round of them in the closing scenes of the 2008 movie. Candace Bushnell, author of the *Sex and the City* books, made it Carrie Bradshaw's signature drink after becoming hooked on them during nights out in New York with, of all people, Bret Easton Ellis (author of *American Psycho*). Cosmos had been doing the rounds long before '90s New York though. A mix of vodka, lime, and grenadine was the drink of choice in San Francisco's gay bars in the 1970s, and this mix was upgraded with cranberry juice and Absolut Citron in the 1980s. It's a crisp, dry, and tangy cocktail. I find it too abrasive made with Absolut Citron, so I've swapped a regular vodka back in. But if you want to mix it just like the *SATC* gang, use a lemon-infused vodka.

Ingredients

1½ ounces vodka

¾ ounce Cointreau

¾ ounce fresh lime juice

¾ ounce cranberry juice

A few dashes of
   orange bitters

Lime twist or wedge,
   to garnish

Instructions

Put a small martini glass into the freezer for 30 minutes, or fill it with ice and set aside to chill.

Pour the vodka, Cointreau, and lime and cranberry juices into a shaker. Half-fill it with ice and dash in some orange bitters, then seal and shake well to chill. Fine-strain into the chilled glass.

Express the lime twist over the cocktail (go to page 15 for a how-to guide), then rub the twist around the rim of the glass. Drop it in to garnish, or discard and garnish with a lime wedge.

Crisp   Dry   Tangy

RAINBOW OVER PARADISE

Making a rainbow-layered cocktail is the closest thing to a magic trick that a bartender can perform. The sight of the different-colored ingredients settling in the glasses, blurring at the edges into greens and oranges but never entirely mixing, always thrills and delights. The secret to getting the layers to work is to vary the viscosity of the ingredients. The more syrupy they are, the more they will sink. In this brightly striped cocktail, the bottom layer is a lusciously thick swirl of grenadine syrup stirred with peach schnapps. Above it floats O.J. that's been mixed with sweetened coconut rum to thicken it up a little. Then on the top, there's a watered-down mix of vodka and blue curaçao. The trio bob along next to each other, creating a rainbow effect that will definitely get a gasp of approval when it's poured. It's an undoubtedly sweet drink, even with the lime juice I've added to try to sharpen it up. If you think it will be too sweet for you, swap the coconut rum for light rum and add an extra ¼ ounce water to the curaçao to keep them apart in the glass.

Ingredients

¾ ounce grenadine syrup
¾ ounce peach schnapps
¾ ounce coconut rum
2½ ounces orange juice
½ ounce fresh lime juice
¼ ounce cold water
¼ ounce blue curaçao
¾ ounce vodka

Instructions

Pour the grenadine and peach schnapps into a hurricane glass and stir briefly to mix. Fill the glass with ice.

Pour the coconut rum, orange juice, and lime juice into a mixing glass. Half-fill with ice and stir for around 30 seconds to chill. Strain slowly into the hurricane glass; the orange layer should float above the grenadine layer.

In a separate, clean glass, mix together the water, blue curaçao, and vodka. Pour it over the bowl of your bar spoon into the glass so the blue layer floats above the orange layer (see page 12 for a guide to floating spirits). Serve straight away.

Fruity   Tropical   Sweet

APEROL SPRITZ

No drink has staged a greater comeback than the Aperol Spritz. Many years ago, in the late nineteenth century, Austrian soldiers in the occupied Veneto region of Italy watered down the local wine with a splash of soda water. They called this a "spritz," after the German word for splash. After the soldiers retreated, the locals kept up the habit of adding soda to their wine, but they also added some booze back in. Bitter amaros, like Campari and Aperol, gave the drinks bite. For a time, the Spritz was local to Venice. And it would probably have stayed that way had the Gruppo Campari not bought Aperol in the early 2000s and decided to introduce it to the world. Savvy event planning and social media campaigning resulted in the Spritz dominating bar culture in every country in which Aperol landed. Every summer people grab their Aperol, a bottle of chilled prosecco, and they embrace the #spritzlife. Nights out, parties, weddings, and celebrations are all orange-hued and fizzily herbal. People even Spritz in the winter at ski resorts now. There's no escaping this Italian aperitif, so if you're down to party you'd better make sure you know how to Spritz.

Ingredients

2 ounces Aperol

3 ounces dry prosecco, chilled

1 ounce soda water, chilled

Orange wheel and olive (optional), to garnish

Instructions

Fill a wine glass with ice. Pour in the Aperol and top up the glass with chilled prosecco.

Stir to mix, then top up the glass with the chilled soda water. Give it a quick stir to just mix the drink. Garnish with an orange wheel, or thread an orange wheel and olive onto a cocktail pick if desired, then drop it into the glass and serve.

Aromatic   Bitter   Fizzy

SPICY MARGARITA

When you want a drink that will chill you out while warming things up, you want a Spicy Margarita. The Spicy Marg is a relatively recent addition to the cocktail hall of greats. The first version of the drink was created in the early 2000s by Julio Bermejo, who owned Tommy's Mexican Restaurant in San Francisco. He started infusing bottles of tequila with habanero peppers and using that fire water to mix Margs. In 2005 a bartender called David Nepove won a cocktail competition at Tommy's with a drink he named the Sweet Heat, which used muddled jalapeños in the mix. Before too long, riffs on the Spicy Marg were popping up everywhere. Some used chile-infused tequila, others muddled in fresh chiles, while chile and fruit pastes were blended into other versions of the drink. This Spicy Margarita uses a homemade Chile Syrup (page 20) for a sugary kiss of heat, as well as a Tajín seasoning rim. Tajín seasoning is a spice mix that's widely available in grocery stores and is made with chiles, lime, and salt, which adds a sour note to the cocktail to make it a drink you'll keep coming back to.

Ingredients

1 lime wedge, plus extra to garnish
A few pinches of Tajín seasoning
1½ ounces reposado tequila
¾ ounce Cointreau
¾ ounce fresh lime juice
½ ounce Chile Syrup (page 20)
Jalapeño slices, to garnish

Instructions

Rub the rim of an old fashioned glass with a lime wedge, then dip it in the Tajín seasoning to lightly coat it. Place it in the freezer for 5–10 minutes to chill.

Half-fill a shaker with ice, then add the tequila, Cointreau, lime juice, and Chile Syrup. Seal and shake well until the tin is frosty.

Fill the chilled glass with crushed ice and strain in the Margarita mix. Drop a few slices of jalapeño chile into the glass, then rest a lime wedge on the rim of the glass to garnish.

Spicy   Tangy   Citrus

PORNSTAR MARTINI

In more genteel parts of the world, this all-conquering modern cocktail is known as the Passion Fruit Martini. It actually began life as the Maverick Martini, named by the drink's inventor, Douglas Ankrah, after the Mavericks Gentlemen's Club in Cape Town. It's a more respectable-sounding name, until you realize that the Maverick is a strip joint. Ankrah decided the name wasn't playful enough for this fruit-fueled cocktail and, on returning to London in 2002, changed it to the Pornstar Martini because he thought that this was the sort of drink a porn star might order. The cheeky name grabbed customers' attentions at Ankrah's bar, The Townhouse in Knightsbridge, and its patisserie-inspired flavors ensured they kept ordering it. Over time the Pornstar Martini has become a bar menu staple and it regularly makes it into the top 10 lists of the world's most popular cocktails.

Ingredients

2 whole passion fruits

2 ounces vanilla vodka

½ ounce passion
    fruit liqueur

¾ ounce passion fruit juice

½ ounce fresh lime juice

½ ounce Simple Syrup
    (page 19)

1½ ounces brut
    Champagne, chilled

Instructions

Pop a coupe glass into the freezer for at least 30 minutes, or fill it with ice and set aside to chill.

Halve the passion fruit and scoop the pulp from 3 of the halves into the shaker (keep the remaining half to garnish). Add the vodka, passion fruit liqueur, passion fruit juice, lime juice, and Simple Syrup. Top up the shaker with ice, seal, and shake really vigorously for 15–30 seconds until chilled.

Fine-strain into the chilled glass. If you're using a cobbler shaker, insert a Hawthorne strainer; the in-built strainer will get gummed up with passion fruit (see page 8 for a guide).

Float the remaining passion fruit half in the Martini and serve with a shot glass of chilled bubbly on the side. You can take alternate sips or pour the Champagne into the Martini before drinking.

Fruity   Tangy   Vanilla

ESPRESSO MARTINI

Rocket fuel for parties, the Espresso Martini has been the bittersweet solution to flagging spirits since the 1980s. Its origin story is one of the best in the cocktail business. It begins in London's Soho Brasserie, an old pub that had been done up to look like a French café. The makeover included the installation of a glamorous marble bar and behind that bar was Dick Bradsell, one of the best barmen in the world. When he wasn't shaking cocktails for Soho's beautiful people, he was sweeping up the coffee grinds that the waiters kept spilling every time they made an espresso. It was annoying, but the smell of coffee combined with the crack of ice every time a shot of vodka got poured gave Dick an idea. So when a famous model (Bradsell never disclosed who) leaned on the bar and asked for a drink that would "wake me up, then **** me up," Dick knew what to do. The original drink was made with a shot of fresh espresso, vodka, Tia Maria, Kahlúa, and Simple Syrup, and Dick called it a Vodka Espresso. Over the years he refined the recipe until he got to the drink we know and love today. When you're making an Espresso Martini at home, you can use either Tia Maria or Kahlúa as the coffee liqueur, or a mix of both. A freshly made espresso is essential; the crema on top of a shot of espresso will give you that iconic layer of foam at the surface of the finished cocktail.

Ingredients
1¾ ounces vanilla vodka
¾ ounce coffee liqueur
¾ ounce hot, fresh espresso
3 coffee beans, to garnish

Instructions
Place a martini or coupe glass into the freezer for at least 30 minutes, or fill it with ice.

Pour the vanilla vodka, coffee liqueur, and espresso into a cocktail shaker. Half-fill it with ice, then seal. Shake really vigorously until the tin is frosty, then strain into the chilled glass (discarding any ice that might have been in it).

Top with 3 coffee beans and serve.

Coffee   Vanilla   Silky

MIDORI MELON SLUSHY

Serves 6

The first time I tried this drink I immediately got brain freeze after slurping too much slushy, too enthusiastically. Like any drink that uses Midori, it has a strong candy store flavor that makes it an incredibly delectable sip. The candied flavor of the musk melons in the Midori is emphasized by the inclusion of frozen cantaloupe melon in the drink. Cantaloupe is actually a type of musk melon, although the Japanese variety is sweeter and juicier than the standard cantaloupe. You can swap in Galia or honeydew melons if you can't get your hands on cantaloupe. As long as the melon leans toward sweet and juicy rather than crisp and refreshing (like watermelon), it would be a good choice to whizz into this bright-green, boozy slushy. This frozen cocktail will start to melt quite quickly, so make it in batches and serve it in chilled glasses to help slow down the thaw. It's a great drink for a summer get-together—a sticky thirst-quencher that's a little bit wild.

Ingredients

14 ounces cantaloupe, peeled and chopped

10½ ounces vodka

4¼ ounces fresh lime juice

7 ounces Midori

3½ ounces Simple Syrup (page 19)

Instructions

Halve the cantaloupe, scoop out the seeds, and then slice away the skin. Roughly chop then transfer to a tray or tub and freeze overnight.

When you're ready to make the slushies, place old fashioned glasses in the freezer to chill. Scoop the frozen cantaloupe into a blender, then pour in the vodka, lime juice, Midori, and Simple Syrup. Add a cupful of ice and blitz until thick and slushy.

Pour into the chilled glasses and serve straight away with reusable straws.

Sherbet   Sweet   Refreshing

SHAMBLES

Serves 6

This outrageous cocktail has appeared on bar menus under a variety of different names, including the VCR (Vodka, Champagne, Red Bull), Chelsea Champagne, and even Liquid Cocaine, due to its supposed ability to wake you up while also messing you up, just like an Espresso Martini (page 84). I've always known it as a Shambles. It's an unholy marriage of crisp French Champagne and the sweet and sour energy drink Red Bull. The combination is full of fizz, literally in the sense of both drinks providing plenty of bubbles, and also in the tangy, tamarind-and-licorice flavors that sparkle in the glass. Red Bull contains a similar amount of caffeine as a cup of coffee, so this cocktail is best kept to the early part of the evening, otherwise you'll find yourself unable to fall asleep when the drinking is done. Although if staying up all night to see the sun rise is part of your plans, this could be the cocktail that carries you through.

Ingredients

7 ounces vodka

7 ounces Red Bull

19 ounces brut
    Champagne, chilled

Lemon slices, to serve

Instructions

Pour the vodka and Red Bull into a mixing glass, then half-fill it with ice. Gently stir for 30–45 seconds to chill.

Fill 6 highballs with ice and strain in the Red Bull mix. Top up with the chilled Champagne and gently stir.

Serve straight away, garnished with lemon slices.

ALTERNATIVE ENERGY DRINKS

If you have another preferred energy drink, feel free to experiment, but bear in mind this will affect the flavor. And always check caffeine levels of drinks and only consume if your body can handle them.

○ Fizzy   ● Tangy   ● Herbal

WOO WOO

Serves 6

Can you put your hands in the air and give me a "woo woo?" Because that's what you're meant to do whenever this zesty, hot-pink cocktail gets poured out. It's supposed to have been invented in the First Edition bar in the Bayside neighborhood of Queens in New York. In the 1980s the bartenders there were big baseball fans and when the New York Mets played the staff would follow the game closely. Every time the Mets scored, the bartenders would shout: "woo woo!" then mix up a batch of this zingy cocktail for everyone in the bar. Glasses lifted in the air, the bar's drinkers would toast the Mets with their own "woo woo!" before enjoying their drink. No surprise, then, that this is a great party cocktail. It's a happy mix of the Cosmopolitan and Fuzzy Navel, with a one–two punch of vodka and peach schnapps combined with a tart, tannic dash of cranberry juice. Easy to mix in a pitcher, refreshingly dry, and a cheerful shade of fuchsia, it's a drink that's hard to resist. Even the most serious of cocktail heads will give in to its crowd-pleasing nature and, ever so quietly, raise a glass and whisper: "woo woo!"

Ingredients

12¼ ounces vodka

6¼ ounces peach schnapps

19 ounces cranberry juice, chilled

A few dashes of peach bitters

Orange or other fresh fruit, to garnish

Instructions

Fill a large pitcher with ice and pour in the vodka, peach schnapps, and cranberry juice. Dash in some peach bitters—around 4–6 shakes should do it. Stir with a long bar spoon for 30–45 seconds to chill.

Serve in ice-filled highball glasses, garnished with orange slices and fresh fruit.

Crisp   Dry   Refreshing

LONG ISLAND ICED TEA

Serves 6

There comes a time in everyone's life, usually in their twenties, when fueling a party with pitchers of Long Island Iced Tea seems like a good idea. Combining a killer mix of rum, gin, vodka, tequila, and Cointreau, it's a cocktail that appeals to people whose idea of a good drink is one with a lot of booze in it. The trouble with this approach is that it usually leads to overconsumption, and what gets forgotten in the aftermath is that this is actually a deliciously punchy cocktail that's worth mixing and enjoying in a more measured fashion. The heat from all those spirits is crisply balanced by the citrus and the spicy sweetness of the cola to create a cooling long drink that would make a good sun-downer on a hot and humid day.

Ingredients

2 ounces light rum

2 ounces London dry gin

2 ounces silver tequila

2 ounces Cointreau

2 ounces vodka

2 ounces fresh lemon juice

2 ounces fresh lime juice

2 ounces Simple Syrup
(page 19)

10½ ounces cola, chilled

Lemon slices, to garnish
(optional)

Instructions

Fill a large pitcher with ice and pour in the rum, gin, tequila, Cointreau, vodka, fresh lemon juice, fresh lime juice, and the Simple Syrup. Stir with a long bar spoon (or wooden spoon) for 30–45 seconds to chill.

Top up the pitcher with the chilled cola and gently stir to mix. Pour into ice-filled highball glasses and garnish with lemon slices, if desired.

Boozy   Crisp   Aromatic

LEMON DROP SHOOTERS

Serves 4

This short version of a Lemon Drop Martini is a punchy vodka shot with a tangy dash of citrus. It tastes like liquored-up lemon sherbet, and it would be fun to roll out at birthday celebrations and brunches. Use a good, mid-tier vodka; you want it to be smooth and creamy enough to blend with the sharp citrus, and not set your throat on fire when you knock it back. If you want to make it extra lemony, use citron vodka instead of plain or, if lemon isn't your favorite citrus, swap the fresh lemon juice for lime, ruby grapefruit, or blood orange juice. If you're making these shooters for a crowd, rim the shot glasses with sugar and then set them in the refrigerator to chill. Shake up several batches of the Lemon Drop mix and transfer it to a bottle or pitcher, ready to pour (the mix does need to be shaken in order to be diluted). Simply top up the glasses and serve.

Ingredients

½ ounce Simple Syrup, plus 1 teaspoon (page 19)

1 teaspoon granulated sugar

1½ ounces vodka

1½ ounces Cointreau

1½ ounces fresh lemon juice

Lemon wedges, to garnish

Instructions

Pour 1 teaspoon of Simple Syrup into a saucer and sprinkle the sugar into a separate saucer. Dip the rim of a shot glass in the syrup, then in the sugar to lightly coat. Repeat with the other glasses. Pop them in the refrigerator to chill for at least 10 minutes to set the sugar rim.

Pour the vodka, Cointreau, and juice into a cocktail shaker and add ½ ounce Simple Syrup. Half-fill with ice. Seal and shake until chilled.

Strain into the shot glasses. Rest a lemon slice on each glass to garnish.

To drink, bite on the lemon wedge, then drink the shot.

Tangy   Citrus   Sherbet

BIRTHDAY CAKE SHOOTERS

Serves 4

When you're celebrating a birthday, you have to have cake. Fun, delicious, and more potent than your average slice of sponge, these dessert-flavored shooters are guaranteed to make your party guests smile. It's a syrupy, creamy, vanilla-scented shot that looks extravagant thanks to a swirl of whipped cream and a good pinch of multicolored sugar sprinkles. To get the best out of this cocktail, make sure you freeze the glasses and fine-strain the cocktail mix when you're pouring it. This will catch any microchips of ice and ensure the drink has a silky texture. Chilling the glasses is important because these shots are tricky to knock back—the heap of whipped cream and sprinkles makes them difficult to slurp down in one go. Instead, sip the liquor through the cream and enjoy the indulgently rich combo of fresh dairy and well-chilled vodka.

Ingredients

1½ ounces vanilla vodka

1½ ounces white crème de cacao

¼ ounce Simple Syrup (page 19)

Whipped cream and cake sprinkles, to garnish

Instructions

Pop the shot glasses into the freezer for 30 minutes to chill.

Pour the vodka, crème de cacao, and Simple Syrup into a shaker and half-fill with ice. Seal and shake vigorously to chill, then fine-strain into the frozen shot glasses.

Top each glass with a squirt of whipped cream (from a can is best) and multicolored sprinkles. Serve straight away.

Creamy   Vanilla   Sweet

HOLY MARY

A Bloody Mary is a brunch essential, but not everyone wants to start the morning after the night before with yet another shot of booze. When you're looking for a zero-proof drink that has enough pep to perk you up, reach for this virgin version of the tomato juice and vodka classic. It is layered with flavor from the homemade Chile Syrup (page 20), generous amounts of Tabasco and Worcestershire sauce, and a good measure of freshly squeezed lime juice. The result is a drink that's hot, sweet, and acidic enough to keep your taste buds interested. If you want to dial down the spice, swap the Chile Syrup for plain Simple Syrup, or simply use less Tabasco. The really important thing is to slide the drink in your cocktail shaker, rather than shaking it, which will ensure the final drink has a deliciously smooth texture.

Ingredients

- 4¼ ounces tomato juice
- ½ ounce fresh lime juice
- ½ ounce Chile Syrup (page 20)
- 4 dashes of Worcestershire sauce
- 5 generous dashes of Tabasco sauce
- 2 pinches of celery salt
- A pinch of freshly ground black pepper
- Lemon wheel and celery stick, to garnish

Instructions

Pour the tomato juice, lime juice, and Chile Syrup into a shaker. Add the Worcestershire sauce, Tabasco, celery salt, and black pepper. Half-fill the shaker with ice. Seal and very gently slide the liquids backwards and forwards in the shaker for around 1 minute to chill them without shaking them (you don't want to end up with frothy tomato juice).

Fill a collins glass with ice and strain in the Holy Mary mix. Garnish with a lemon wheel and a celery stick and serve.

Spicy   Sweet   Tangy

WALK ON THE BEACH

Serves 2

I love a Piña Colada, but there are times when I don't want the gentle buzz of a shot of rum but do still want to enjoy the tropical flavors and rich, velvety texture of that classic beach cocktail. On those occasions I reach for this zero-proof version. It's made with a combination of pineapple chunks and juice blended together with coconut milk which gives the drink a thick, slurpable consistency that makes it so satisfying. The Demerara Syrup (page 19) adds a fudgy flavor while the lime juice sharpens everything up. It's a soft drink that looks, feels, and tastes good, so no one will think they're missing out by drinking an alcohol-free cocktail. If the weather is really hot and you want to turn it into popsicles, use 3½ ounces Demerara Syrup and freeze overnight in popsicle molds.

Ingredients

5¼ ounces pineapple chunks, drained

7 ounces pineapple juice

3½ ounces coconut milk

2 ounces fresh lime juice

1 ounce Demerara Syrup (page 19)

Maraschino cherries and fresh pineapple wedges, to garnish

Instructions

Scoop the pineapple chunks into a blender. Pour in the pineapple juice, coconut milk, lime juice, and Demerara Syrup. Add 4 cups of ice and blitz until smooth and foamy.

Pour into 2 hurricane or poco grande glasses. Garnish with maraschino cherries and pineapple wedges and serve with reusable straws.

Tropical   Creamy   Coconut

DISCO SHANDY

When it comes to zero-proof drinks, my two favorites are Crodino and alcohol-free lager, so combining them to make a mocktail is a no-brainer. Crodino is a nonalcoholic Italian aperitivo. It's a slightly syrupy alternative to amaros, like Campari and Aperol, and it has the same multilayered, herbal flavor that brims with woody herbs, spice, and citrus. In Italy it's served over ice in a wine glass with a slice of orange, but I find it a little too sugary by itself. I think it's at its best lengthened out with soda, a nonalcoholic prosecco to make a booze-free Spritz, or mixed with a hoppy, zero-proof beer to make a tangy alcohol-free shandy. Of course, if you do want to add some liquor back in, you can just use a regular lager. With or without alcohol, the drink will have the same zippy hit of flavor and cheerful, sunset-orange hue.

Ingredients

3½ ounces Crodino, chilled

7 ounces alcohol-free lager, chilled

Lemon slice, to garnish

Instructions

About 30 minutes before you want to make the Shandy, pop a collins or beer glass into the refrigerator to chill.

When you're ready, pour the Crodino into the frosted glass, then top up with the chilled alcohol-free lager. Garnish with a lemon slice and serve.

Aromatic   Herbal   Refreshing

SHIRLEY TEMPLE

Disco Drinks

The queen of the mocktails, the Shirley Temple is named after the 1930s movie actor, who somehow starred in 42 films before the age of 22. This alcohol-free cocktail was created especially for Shirley by a bartender at Chasen's Restaurant in Beverly Hills, a joint where many an Oscar party was held. Being a child star, Shirley would go to Hollywood parties but, of course, she couldn't drink alcohol and she complained about feeling left out when the drinks were handed round and there was nothing she could sip on. So the Shirley Temple was created, and it's been a mainstay with nondrinkers ever since. The crisp combination of ginger ale and lime juice is sweetened up with a dash of grenadine. If, unlike Shirley, you can drink alcohol and want to, then you can turn this into a Dirty Shirley by adding a shot of vodka and a dash of cherry brandy.

128

Ingredients
½ ounce grenadine syrup

½ ounce fresh lime juice

5½ ounces ginger ale, chilled

Maraschino cherry, to garnish

Instructions
Fill a highball glass with ice and pour in the grenadine syrup and lime juice. Stir to mix.

Top up with the ginger ale and stir. Garnish with a maraschino cherry.

Crisp   Dry   Refreshing

PINEAPPLE AND CREAM SODA

Finding zero-proof drinks for people who like to party without the buzz of booze has got much easier over the years, but there is still a tendency for alcohol-free drinks to lean heavily on sugar to make up for the lack of liquor. I'm not against sugar, but sometimes your teeth do start to itch when you're on a night out with your friends and the fourth or fifth syrupy soft drink appears on the table. It's hard to have fun when there's the worry of dentist bills to come. This old-fashioned cream soda uses the natural sweetness of pineapple juice to create a grownup mocktail that's briskly refreshing while indulgent enough to feel like a treat. It has a subtle, fruity flavor, but if you'd like a stronger hit of pineapple, size up your glass and use 3½ ounces pineapple juice. If pineapple isn't your favorite flavor of fruit, try making this mocktail with orange juice, grapefruit juice, or a luxurious splash of passion fruit purée.

Ingredients
2 ounces pineapple juice

3½ ounces soda water, chilled

¾ ounce light cream

Pineapple wedge, to garnish

Instructions
Fill a highball glass with ice and pour in the pineapple juice and soda water. Stir to mix.

Pour the cream into the glass, then gently stir to ripple the cream through the soda. Garnish the glass with a pineapple wedge and serve.

Creamy   Fruity   Indulgent/Luxurious

LEMON, LIME, AND SODA

Serves 2

The secret to making things disco is to take something normal and ordinary and then go a bit extra with it. For example, take lime and soda. For many years a large glass of lime and soda was my soberista drink of choice at the bar. Less sugary than a cola and more grownup than an orange juice, it was a fresh and thirst-quenching drink. But also a little boring. I still love the combination of sharp lime and the sour fizz of soda water, but I want to make it more fun. The obvious way to take it to the next level is to give the drink a dessert makeover and add a scoop of zesty lemon sorbet, which gives the drink texture and sweetens while it chills. Using a combination of fresh lime juice and lime cordial adds crispness, and the resulting drink is like a lemonade plus. It tastes of summer and al fresco dates in pub gardens, when the sun is shining and all is good in the world.

Ingredients

2 generous scoops of lemon sorbet

1¾ ounces fresh lime juice

1¾ ounces lime cordial

Chilled soda water, to top up

Mint sprigs and lemon wedges (optional), to garnish

Instructions

Drop a scoop of lemon sorbet into each of 2 collins glasses, then pour in the lime juice and lime cordial. Top up the glasses with chilled soda water. You'll need to tilt the glasses as your pour, so you're pouring the soda water down the side of the glass rather than directly onto the sorbet. The soda will foam up, so do this slowly. You may need to half-fill the glass with soda, then let the bubbles die down before filling it up.

Garnish with mint sprigs and lemon wedges, if desired. Serve straight away with spoons or reusable straws.

Refreshing   Citrus   Cooling

ANGEL WINGS

If you love the rich taste of dairy but can't or don't want to indulge in a drink layered with cream or ice cream, then this mocktail could be the beverage for you. It's made with a measure of Vanilla Syrup (page 20), which immediately gives it an ice-cream parlor flavor. A generous dash of passion fruit juice and a sharp shot of fresh lime juice makes a tart and sweet combination that takes this faux cream soda somewhere tropical. It reminds me of the juice drinks that used to be popular when I was little, full of faraway fruit flavors and the promise of endless sunshine and days full of play. This is a luxurious soft drink that would make a great zero-proof option at formal parties. Mix the syrup, lime juice, and passion fruit together and chill for a few hours, then mix with the soda water in pitchers, ready to pour when your guests arrive.

Ingredients

1¼ ounces Vanilla Syrup (page 20)

¾ ounce fresh lime juice

2 ounces passion fruit juice

3½ ounces soda water, chilled

Passion fruit wedge, to garnish

Instructions

Fill a collins glass with ice cubes. Pour in the Vanilla Syrup, lime juice, and passion fruit juice and gently stir to mix. Top up with chilled soda water and stir a couple of times.

Rest a passion fruit wedge on top of the ice. Serve with a reusable straw.

 Indulgent/Luxurious   Fruity   Vanilla

PINK LEMONADE

Serves 4

When you want a zero-proof drink that's guaranteed to cheer you up, think pink. This classic lemonade is made by blending lemon and orange juices together with Simple Syrup, then it's given extra pizazz by blitzing in a few handfuls of fresh raspberries (or frozen raspberries, if you want to instantly chill the drink). The result is a cheerfully pink syrup with a zippy hit of citrus that you can dilute with iced still or seltzer water, depending on how fizzy you like your lemonade. It's a juicy drink that's full of the joys of summer, and you can mix it up depending on what fruit you have on hand. Strawberries, blueberries, blackberries, chopped peaches, apricots, or nectarines would all make a good sub for the raspberries. Dedicate your summer to trying them all out until you find the fruit lemonade that makes you smile the most. When you find it, keep it alcohol-free or try mixing it with a dash of rum. Perfect for afternoons spent sipping drinks in the garden or on the porch.

Ingredients   **Instructions**

WHIPPED LEMONADE

Serves 4

When a drink starts trending on TikTok, it's always worth taking note. In the summer of 2021, the viral drink of choice was Whipped Lemonade. It's a lusciously thick drink made with fresh lemon juice, condensed milk, and whipping cream that undoubtedly owes its origins to Brazilian Lemonade, a creamy soft drink that's made by blending whole limes, condensed milk, and sugar. Using just juice rather than whole fruit means you don't need a super-strong blender to whizz the drink together, and you can even make it in a bowl with a hand-held milk frother. This will whip in extra air, making the lemonade lighter and foamier. Serve it simply garnished with citrus and fresh herbs or, to make it extra indulgent, top off the lemonade with an extra swirl of whipped cream.

Ingredients

8¾ ounces whipping cream

3 ounces condensed milk

3 ounces fresh lemon juice

Lime wheels and mint
    sprigs, to garnish

Instructions

Pour the whipping cream, condensed milk, and lemon juice into a blender. Add 4 cups of ice and blend until smooth and creamy.

Pour into 4 highball or tulip glasses. Garnish each glass with a lime wheel and mint sprig and serve with reusable straws.

Creamy   Citrus   Indulgent/Luxurious

CHERRY COKE FLOAT

Serves 4

Is there anything more nostalgic than an ice cream float? Even if you didn't drink ice cream sodas during school vacation when you were growing up, somehow the second a frothy glass of cola and ice cream is served up you'll find yourself transported back in time to when you were a kid and the most important things in your life were your friends, being allowed out to ride your bike, and getting your hands on as much soda pop as possible. Cherry coke was first rolled out in 1985, making this an extra-nostalgic drink for anyone who longs for a *Stranger Things* childhood (minus the Demogorgon). When you pour your cherry-flavored cola into the glass with the vanilla ice cream, it will immediately foam up, creating a fluffy layer of froth that will crown your ice cream soda. To keep the froth down to a manageable level, trickle the cola down the side of the glass so you steadily build a layer of foam rather than a fizzing spume of bubbles that flows over the top of the glass.

Ingredients

2 ounces grenadine syrup

2 ounces tart cherry juice

3 cups (24 ounces) cola, chilled

4 large scoops of vanilla ice cream

Whipped cream and maraschino cherries, to garnish

Instructions

Pour the grenadine syrup and tart cherry juice into a pitcher. Stir well to mix. Pour in the cola and gently stir to combine.

Add large scoops of vanilla ice cream to 4 mason or collins glasses. Top up the glasses with the chilled cherry cola. You'll need to tilt the glasses as you pour, so you're pouring the cola down the side of the glass rather than directly onto the ice cream. The cola will foam up, so do this slowly. You may need to half-fill each glass with cola, then let the bubbles die down before filling them up.

Top the drink with a spoonful of whipped cream, a maraschino cherry, and a reusable straw, to stir.

Creamy   Fizzy   Aromatic

ARNOLD PALMER

Serves 4

Every country, even the booziest, has its favorite alcohol-free sipper. In America, it's sweet tea. Southern sweet tea is made by brewing black tea and sweetening it with Simple Syrup. It's a refreshing combination, but if you prefer your soft drinks with a little sparkle, you'll want to try an Arnold Palmer. The drink is named after the legendary golfer, who asked for his iced tea to be mixed with lemonade after a long, hot day designing a golf course in Palm Springs. A woman sitting by his table heard his drinks order and asked the waitress to make her one of those Arnold Palmer drinks. Palmer was such a hero and an influence that soon everyone in the club was ordering Arnold Palmer drinks and the trend quickly spread to golf clubs across the States. Proof, if proof were needed, that where one trendsetter goes, everyone else will follow. Palmer ended up going into the beverage business and selling bottled Arnold Palmers, ready to drink. But they're easy to mix at home. You just need freshly boiled water, a pitcher, some patience, and plenty of ice.

Ingredients

¼ ounce black tea leaves or 3 tea bags

5 cups (40 ounces) sparkling lemonade, chilled

Lemon wedges, to garnish

Instructions

Place the tea in a heatproof pitcher and cover with 3 ½ cups (28 ounces) of freshly boiled water. Let it steep for 5–6 minutes, then strain the tea into a clean pitcher and set aside to cool for at least 30 minutes.

Fill 4 highball glasses with ice and pour 4¼ ounces of tea into each glass. Top up with the chilled lemonade. Drop lemon wedges into the glasses to garnish and serve with a reusable straw.

Aromatic   Citrus   Herbal

ABOUT THE AUTHOR

Jassy Davis is a cocktail gal. She has previously written five books dedicated to mixing drinks, including *Gin Made Me Do It*, *Mocktails Made Me Do It*, *Winter Warmers*, *Summer Sparklers*, and *Party Pops!* When she does put down her cocktail shaker, she enjoys developing recipes for brands that like their dishes to be cozy and comforting with a dash of fun. She lives by the sea in Brighton, England, and you can find her on Instagram at @ginandcrumpets.

PICTURE CREDITS

All listed in alphabetical order

Cover: front cover: **Yulia Glam/ Shutterstock.com** (disco frame); **Walter Pfisterer/Stockfood.co.uk** (cocktail) Spine: **muratart/Shutterstock.com** (disco ball) Back cover: **Ron Dale/Shutterstock.com** (background glitter); **New Africa/ Shutterstock.com**; **etorres/ Shutterstock.com** (mid cocktail); **Ivan Mateev/Shutterstock.com** (bottom cocktail)

Endpapers: **Angel McNall Photography/ Shutterstock.com**

Interior:
100%OperaFotografica/AdobeStock. com: 61
3523studio/Shutterstock.com: 26, 61
Alexander Prokopenko/Shutterstock. com: 94
Andreas Argirakis/Shutterstock.com: 73
Anton Lyaskovskyy/Shutterstock.com: 41
Arina P Habich/Shutterstock.com: 109
Artiom Photo/Shutterstock.com: 22
Blachkovsky/Shutterstock.com: 8
Brent Hofacker/Shutterstock.com: 3, 30, 38, 42, 46, 49, 65, 70, 81, 126, 129, 137
Casther/Shutterstock.com: 16
Clash and Clash/Shutterstock.com: 4, 93

Dace Kundrate/Alamy.com: 141
Dee-n/Shutterstock.com: 134
Dementieva Iryna/Shutterstock.com: 138
DenisMArt/Shutterstock.com: 53
Diana Taliun/Shutterstock.com: 9
didesign021/Shutterstock.com: 57
domnitsky/Shutterstock.com: 14, 14
Eatyurvegtables/Shutterstock.com: 3, 45
Ekaterina_Molchanova/Shutterstock. com: 3, 62, 77
Elena Veselova/Shutterstock.com: 142
etorres/Shutterstock.com: 11, 25
Evgeny Karandaev/Shutterstock.com: 6
Fernanda Flugel/Shutterstock.com: 58
Food Impressions/Shutterstock.com: 29
Francesco Italia/AdobeStock.com: 113
gwozdeff/Shutterstock.com: 117
Hitdelight/Shutterstock.com: 118
Ivan Mateev/Shutterstock.com: 18, 74, 102
Jacqui Caulton: 121
James Yardley/Shutterstock.com: 54
JeniFoto/Shutterstock.com: 94
Johann/AdobeStock.com: 101, 107
KaiMook Studio 99/Shutterstock.com: 110, 141
Katarzyna Hurova/Shutterstock.com: 73, 93, 107, 121, 142
Kondor83/Shutterstock.com: 12
Lifestyle Travel Photo/Shutterstock. com: 130
LoveYouStock/Shutterstock.com: 46, 62, 113
Madlen/Shutterstock.com: 17
Mark Chandler Photography/ Shutterstock.com: 21
Master1305/Shutterstock.com: 27–143, 144
Mayatnikstudio/AdobeStock.com: 37
Medolka/Shutterstock.com: 98
Micaela Fiorellini/Shutterstock.com: 89
Milanchikov Sergey/Shutterstock.com: 122

Muratart/Shutterstock.com: 1, 6, 8–22, 144
Nature's Charm/Shutterstock.com: 69
New Africa/Shutterstock.com: 6, 66, 125
Oksana Mizina/Shutterstock.com: 34, 105
Pixel-Shot/Shutterstock.com: 7
Plateresca/Shutterstock.com: 97
popout/Shutterstock.com: 50
ridersuperone/Shutterstock.com: 90
Ron Dale/Shutterstock.com: 6
Scott Near/Shutterstock.com: 85
Sean Ware/Shutterstock.com: 114
Simplylove/Shutterstock.com: 33, 70
Snowbelle/Shutterstock.com: 10
surachet khamsuk/Shutterstock.com: 41, 69, 89, 125, 129
TanyaFox/Shutterstock.com: 5
Tati Liberta/Shutterstock.com: 133
Tim UR/Shutterstock.com: 15
Valeriia Horovets/Shutterstock.com: 78
Vidic Bojan/Shutterstock.com: 2
Vladimir Sukhachev/Shutterstock.com: 19
White Tusk Studios/Shutterstock. com: 82
WITTY/AdobeStock.com: 110
Wollertz/Shutterstock.com: 33
Yevheniia/AdobeStock.com: 2
Yousefsh/Shutterstock.com: 86
Yulia Glam/Shutterstock.com: 4, 25, 74, 101, 122, 137